EDUCATIONAL INTEREST
AND
INTELLECTUAL COMMITMENT

Educational Interest and Intellectual Commitment

By

Darshana P. Sharma

ANMOL PUBLICATIONS PVT. LTD.
NEW DELHI - 110 002 (INDIA)

ANMOL PUBLICATIONS PVT. LTD.
4374/4B, Ansari Road, Daryaganj
New Delhi - 110 002
Ph.: 23261597, 23278000
Visit us at: www.anmolpublications.com

Educational Interest and Intellectual Commitment

First Published, 2004

ISBN 81-261-1953-5

PRINTED IN INDIA

Published by J.L. Kumar for Anmol Publications Pvt. Ltd., New Delhi - 110 002 and Printed at Mehra Offset Press, Delhi.

Contents

Preface

In India, under the 10+2+3 structure of education, general education is imparted to the children for the first ten years. This education is common to all the children in the country. At class eleven students make choice of the courses to be studied. The objective of Plus Two stage is to provide students with an opportunity to acquire the specialised knowledge and skills needed to participate in the task of national reconstruction. For preparing manpower required for this purpose, one important consideration to be kept in mind is the basic differences in the abilities and other attributes of individuals that make some individuals more suitable for specific fields of work than the others. In order that an individual may be able to achieve the targets he is capable of achieving, it is essential that he follows appropriate courses of study as per his interest but at the same time has a level of intellectual commitment commensurating with that.

Educational interest and intellectual commitment donot work in isolation. There are certain cognitive and non-cognitive factors which influence the both. The knowledge of bearing of certain personality characteristics, mental ability, level of intellectual commitment, academic achievement, emotional stability and socio-economic status is significant for educational and vocational guidance. The knowledge of predictors of success in academic courses too is significant for avoiding wastage of resources.

The research work on which this book is based investigated into the educational interest and intellectual commitment of students grouped into different categories. The study also examined the relationship of educational interest with subject-wise and total academic achievement of high school students and relationship of educational interest with socio-economic status, intellectual commitment and intelligence besides determining predictors of academic achievement.

The book has been divided into six chapters. The first chapter on theoretical background of the problem deals with the significance of the study, history of measurement of interest, statement of problem, conceptual framework, objectives, hypotheses and the delimitations of the study.

The second chapter reviews some of the studies conducted in India and abroad on educational/vocational interest patterns followed by studies related to educational/vocational interest and intelligence, interest and academic achievement and interest and socio-economic status.

The chapter three delineates the design of the study wherein the method, sampling, tools, procedure for data collection, scoring and techniques used for statistical analysis have been briefly explained.

The analysis and discussion of results, constituting major part of the study have been reported in chapter four and five. These chapters deal with the nature of educational interest and intellectual commitment scores, educational interest patterns of students grouped into different categories, the significance of difference in the mean scores of educational interest and intellectual commitment, relationship of each of the seven areas of educational interest with the subject-wise and total academic achievement, relationship of educational interest with socio-economic status, intellectual commitment and intelligence, and prediction of academic achievement of high school boys and girls on the basis of introversion, extraversion, socio-economic status, intellectual commitment, intelligence and adjustment.

The last and sixth chapter is devoted to the derivation of conclusions, educational implications of the findings and suggestions for further research.

This piece of research was planned and conducted to fill much needed gap in the area of educational interest and intellectual commitment. Needless to mention that however, precise techniques be used, an attempt of this kind may not claim to be final and as such, it should be seen in the light of the delimitations stated. I hope this work would make a humble contribution to the body of knowledge.

I wish to put on record the contributions of all those by whose encouragements and efforts the book has come out in its present form. I express my deep sense of gratitude to Dr. Lokesh K. Verma, Professor, Department of Education, University of Jammu for his scholarly supervision and inspiring guidance in carrying out the research study. I owe my thanks to Prof. S.P. Suri, Prof. Kiran Sumbli Prof. N.R. Sharma, Prof. Aruna Suri and Late Prof. Meenakshi Chopra for their valuable suggestions on the research work. I also take the opportunity to express my sincere thanks to Prof. N.S. Mavi, Faculty of Education, Kurukshetra University, Kurukshetra for his inspiration, encouragement and valuable directions to carry out this work. I cannot forget the help rendered to me by the members of the staff of NCERT Library, and NIEPA Library, New Delhi and Central Library, Panjab University, Chandigarh. I acknowledge my gratitude to all of them.

I wish to put on record the help and cooperation that came from my husband Dr. Rajendra P. Sharma, daughter Ananya and son Apoorv.

Last but not the least, I express my thanks to Anmol Publications Pvt. Ltd., New Delhi for gladly publishing this book.

Darshana P. Sharma

1

Introduction

Education as a process has to cater to the needs of national development. The task of national development involves exploitation of physical and human resources and demands long-range concerted planned efforts on the part of all organs of the whole societal system. Education is one sub-system which can contribute in a significant way in these endeavours. The major contribution is that it can prepare personnel with upto-date knowledge and skills along with certain desirable personal attributes, to make them useful individuals in different fields of work in the society. For preparing personnel for these varied fields, one important consideration to be kept in mind is the basic differences in the abilities and other attributes of human individuals that make certain individuals more suitable for specific fields of work than others. Such differences, however, start appearing at an early age of the individual. Therefore, the educational system has to take into cognizance these differences right at the school stage, and utillize them to the maximum for the benefit of individual and society. Knowing the direction and magnitude of differences in human beings is very essential so as to devise strategies for diversification and selection of persons for various training and work situations. The 'Doctrine of Individual Differences' emphasizes that individuals differ in the degree to which they possess about any characteristic that can be named and in the total pattern of their personality. But how to draw the maximum benefit of this impact. It can be only through good measuring instruments by which students can be differentiated. Strong, E.K. Jr. says "An achievement test does this to a degree after the student has taken the required courses.... Aptitude and interest tests are more useful than achievement tests, since they can be employed before and not after the course has been taken up." Terman pointed out the importance of interest study with a view that "for understanding an individual's total personality it is absolutely necessary to know something about the kinds and intensity of his interests. As long as this knowledge is lacking, neither educational, nor vocational guidance can have a solid foundation." Thus due consideration and measurement of interests are something indispensable in educational and vocational fields. It is in this context that measurement of interest is of special significance.

Moreover, certain personality characteristics, intellectual level, level of intellectual commitment, level of achievement, emotional stability as well as socio-economic status are of significance in individual's life when he has to make a choice either for his course of study or for work. At higher Secondary stage the child is to make selection of subjects according to the vocation he chooses for his/her future life, because this is the stage after which choice of subjects is not possible. A higher secondary school runs different streams and child should make selection of streams according to his/her abilities, interests and aptitudes. The economic and social status of the family have some effect on the choice of subjects of their children. Literate families render more guidance to their children than illiterate families. When parents and siblings are literate, they would guide their children and younger siblings for appropriate choice according to their interests and aptitudes. Wrong choice of subjects is likely to lead to wastage of human resources and manpower. In order that an individual may be able to achieve the targets he is capable of achieving, it is essential that he follows appropriate courses of study, and for this students need assistance from the teachers, guidance workers and parents. Most of the students have high aspirations but have no knowledge of their capacities, interests and economic status. Hence they are not realistic in their choices. There is wastage of human energy without adequate educational and vocational guidance.

In the recommendations of Secondary Education Commission (1952-53). "The provision of diversified courses of instruction imposes on teachers and school administrators the additional responsibility of giving proper guidance to pupils in their choice of courses and careers." Indian Education Commission (1964-66) re-emphasized the need of realization of the fucntions of guidance. "One of the main functiosn of guidance at the secondary level is to aid in the identification and development of the abilities and interests of adolescent pupils. It helps these pupils to understand their own strengths and limitations and to do scholastic work at the level of their ability; to gain information about educational and vocational opportunities and requirements; to make realistic educational and vocational choices and plans based on a consideration of all relevant factors; and to find solution to their problems of personal and social adjustment in the school and home." The research and other relevent literature in India and abroad suggests that subject choices at secondary level are products of a number of interesting factors: utility, easiness, availability in the schools, previous achievement, perception of success, social prestige of course, parents, advice, the economic aspect of educational courses etc. The pupils interests and abilities as well as teachers wield a strong influence in subject choices.

Study of relationships between interest, intellectual commitment, intelligence and achievement is necessary for educational and vocational guidance. All these are to be taken into consideration before a student selects a particular course of study. In this complex social structure of society of today, choosing a career or vocation in life can not be left uncared for. The complexity and specialization in all fields of human endeavour have created the problem of proper selection of career. There are numerous branches and sub-branches which require special abilities, personality traits and interest to pursue them successfully. The knowledge of correlations enables the teacher to predict the child's behaviour and his future attainments. Hence, there is need of testing the interest and then to correlate it with the abilities one possesses, level of commitment one is having and achievement one has made to ensure for smooth running with the profession and to avoid him to be a misfit.

Moreover, educational administrators today are faced with the most challenging problem of accurate prediction of future success of students in academic courses. There are many students who pass the examination, yet they fail to achieve as much as they could have in terms of their abilities. Many parents and teachers have the concept that the failing students lack intelligence. But the fact is that the failing students have sufficient intelligence but they are unable to achieve the desired level of success due to certain non-cognitive factors such as interest, socio-economic status, self concept, personality make-up and adjustment. They may not be clear about their likings and abilities, may be mal-adjusted or some socio-economic handicaps may be creating hindrances in the achievement of maximum of their abilities. If definite predictors of academic success are known precisely, it may be possible to guide the students to select those courses in which they have maximum ability of achieving success.

Measurement of Interests

Informal observations about the individual differences in interests date back to at least as early as Plato's comment in '*The Republic*' (book-II) that "No two individuals are born exactly alike but each differs from each in natural endowments, one being suited for one occupation and another for another." Interest inventories have progressed a great deal from the initial attempts of G. Stanley Hall in 1907 to develop a questionnaire to measure children's cultural interests. The pioneer work on the conceptualization and measurement of interests is usually attributed to Walter V. Bingham and his colleagues at Carnegie Institute of Technology, where Bingham established the Institute of Applied Psychology in 1915. It was there that James Burt (1922) developed a questionnaire to assist students in their vocational choices which included some of the first interest items ever devised; that Bruce N. Moore (1921) successfully differentiated the interest of design and sales engineers and that C.S. Yoakim and his students experimented with the interests measures in the selection and training of salesmen.

Although measurement of interests was of concern prior to

1920s, the first formal, scientific and orderly approach to the study and measurement of interests began in 1919. In a graduate seminar on interests, conducted at the Carnegic Institute of Technology, students and professors developed items to distinguish between members of different occupations. Many inventories evolved from the seminar, the most notable being the Strong Vocational Interest Blank (SVIB). In constructing the original SVIB, two innovations to the measurement of interests were introduced: (i) The items dealt with a subject's likes and dislikes, and the responses were empirically keyed for the different occupational groups. It was not until 1939 that another standardised inventory known as Kuder Preference Record was Published. In 1948, Guilford Interest Survey was published. Two unique features of this inventory were the use of factor analysis in the refinement of various scales and separate scores for vocational and avocational interests. In 1959, the Giest Picture Inventory was published. The Minnesota Vocational Interest Inventory (MVII), published in 1965, is useful for high school students who are occupational bound rather than college bound. In 1969, the Ohio Vocational Interest Survey, (OVIS), which, like the MVII, is based upon occupations described in the Dictionary of Occupational Titles was published.

In India, most of the work was done in the area of measuring general or vocational interests rather than measuring educational interests. Chatterjee's Non-language preference record, Jabalpur Interest Inventory, Hafeez Interest Test, Pandey Interest Test, Singh Interest Record, Kulshretha's Interest Parisuchi, Vocational Interest of Madami, Bhardwaj's Occupational and Avocational Interest Record; all these cover either general or vocational interests. The Interest Parisuchi Published by Messers Psychological Corporation and Kulshretha's Educational Interest Record published by National Psychological Corporation were the only available educational interest tests.

Statement of the Problem

Most of the work in India and abroad was done in the area of general and vocational interests. There was dearth of tests in the area of educational interest required for educational guidance. Hence there was need for constructing an educational interest inventory. Realising the magnitude of the problem, the investigator decided to construct an educational interest inventory on the pattern of Strong Vocational Interest Blank and to relate educational interest and intellectual commitment with certain cognitive and non-cognitive variables. The problem was stated as :

"Intellectual Commitment and Educational Interest in Relation to certain Cognitive and Non-Cognitive Variables.

Meaning of the Variables Undertaken

There were many variables incorporated in formulating the problem. It was essential to be clear to each of those. The following were the variables involved :

Interest

Informal observations of individual differences in interest date back at least as early as Plato's comment in 'The Republic' that "No two persons are alike but each differs from each in natural endowments, one being suited for one occupation and other for other". He further says, "knowledge which is acquired under compulsion obtains no hold over the mind- then do not use compulsion, but let early education be a sort of amusement, you will then be better able to find out the natural bent". Thus interest is a primary motivating force in life.

Interests are traits of Personality of an individual which are significant for satisfaction and success in the educational and vocational fields. These traits are manifested as likes and dislikes, preferences and indifferences. A phenomenon of acceptance and rejection is involved in the issue of likes and disslikes. The objects, activities or experimences which command our interest are stimulating, enjoyable and pleasurable, whereas the opposite is true in case of our dislikes. The phenomenonof interests involve choosing the most acceptable alternative out of many, going after preferred objects, activities etc. and consequently deriving satisfaction, success and happiness out of one's interests. There seems to be something magnetic about interests, pulling people in their direction and holding them in place once there.

Everyone possesses certain interests due to which he likes certain activities and dislikes others. Thus, interest means to make a difference. It describes why the organism tends to favour some situations and then comes to react to them in a very selective manner.

Interest is a matter of giving keen attention to something- an object, an activity or an idea. Interest can be the cause of an activity and result of participation in that activity. Interest is one of the important factors in motivating the acquisition of knowledge, information and skills. It is a drive that leads a person to decide his preferences. A person interested in an object implies that he becomes curious to know it, pays attention to it and learns more about it.

In a *Comprehensive Dictionary of Psychology and Psycho analytical terms,* English and English (1958) have stated that interest is a term of elusive meanings, and they give several meanings of interest. The first meaning is in terms of 'an attitude' or 'a set of attending.' The second meaning regards interest as 'the tendency to give selective attention to something.' In the third meaning, an interest is regarded as 'an attitude or a feeling that an object or an event makes a difference or is of concern to oneself.' The fourth meaning of interest is in terms of 'striving to be fully aware of a character of an object.' The fifth meaning of interest is 'the feeling without which a person is unable to learn.' The sixth meaning of interest emphasizes 'a pleasurable feeling that accompanies an activity proceeding unhindered towards the goal.' The seventh meaning of interest is in terms of 'a tendency to engage in an activity solely for the gratification of engaging therein.' Thus varied meanings can be attached to term 'interest.'

Definitions of Interest

It is not easy to furnish a definition of interest that shall at the same time conform to technical and scientific requirements and be applicable to the problems of educational and vocational guidance. The word itself had a long popular history before it was adopted for scientific usage, and, as in the case of words intelligence and character, some confusion has arisen from the mixture of the scientific and the popular.

Writers have defined interests as pre-occupations, objectives, likes, dislikes and motives. When interests are plotted as patterns or profiles, they are located on a scale ranging from non-interest or zero point to a high positive value. From the operational point of view, it is sufficient to look upon interests as organismic conditions that result in a desire for further stimulations from a particular type of object, idea or experiences.

Woodworth (1918) says, "From the introspective side, an interest is somewhat similar to an emotion; from the side of behaviour, it is a drive towards an activity of the capacity to which it is attached".

According to Strong (1943) "Interest scores measure a complex of liked and disliked activities equivalent to a condition which supplies stimulation for a particular type of behaviour. Interest scores are consequently measures of drives". Thus according to Strong, "interests are activities for which we have liking and disliking and which we go toward or away from or concerning which we at least continue or discontinue the status quo."

McDougall (1949), the famous English psychologist, gave a psychological interpretation of interest and defined it thus "An interest is a form of activity for which we have taste and which is also sustained by a sentiment."

Saviskas (1999) states, "Interests expedite person-environment interactions by uniting subject, object and behaviour into a vital relationship that satisfies needs, fulfills values, forters self development, enhances adaptation and substantiates indentity. Blustein and Flum (1999) define interests as a "central effective synthesis, that assimilates these exploratory experiences into a coherent sense of self. Thus interests link personal needs and environmental action."

From the definitions given so far, it is inferred that interests are the factors that attract an individual to or repel him from objects, persons and activities. Interest is a tendency to make consistent choices in a certain direction without external pressures and in the face of alternatives, i.e. it represents the tendency to select certain activities or things in preference to certain others. The success in a course of study or a job depends not only on the ability of the individual but also depends on his/her interests.

Educational Interest

Educational interest is defined as one's own pattern of preferences, likes and dislikes preferred in any manner, wisely or unwisely by self, or by another source for a given educational area or subject. It reflects choices of the students for various subjects of study.

Educational interests are of considerable importance in exploiting the human resource potential for national development. Not only this, educational interests are important even in the development of an individual as study of subjects compatible with one's interests leads to satisfaction and happiness in life.

The educational interest plays very significant role in educational guidance, which is a process of helping a student to develop or accept an integrated and adequate picture of himself and a clear understanding of his problems, and of his role in the world of education (school and college), with satisfaction to himself and benefit to school and society.

Intellectual Commitment

Intellectual commitment owes its origin to job involvement. To have a clear understanding of the concept of intellectual commitment, it is first of all necessary to be clear to the concept of job involvement.

In the social science literature of the past four decades, one encounters very often the concept of involvement. The strong impact of Marx, Weber and Durkheim is quite evident in the contemporary writings on the subject of involvement. Dubin (1975) defined involvement as central life interest. According to him, a job involved person is one who considers work to be the most important part of his life and engages in it as an end in itself. Faunce (1959) also considers job involvement as commitment to job in which success performance is regarded an end in itself rather than means to an end.

In trying to explain the nature of job involvement, psychologists have concentrated on the analysis of specific motivational states of the individual in work situations. Vroom (1962) proposed that a person's attempt to satisfy his or her needs for self esteem through work on the job leads to job involvement. Vroom seems to emphasize intrinsic need satisfaction as the essential condition for higher job involvement.

Lodahl and Kejner (1965) proposed two definitions of job involvement. One of their definitions states that job involvement is the degree to which a person is identified psychologically with his work, or the importance of work in his total self- image. Such a psychological state of identification with work may result partly from early socialization training during which an individual may internalize the value of goodness of work. They also provided another definition of job involvement. This definition states that the job involvement is the degree to which a person's work performance effects his self- esteem.

Lawler and Hall (1970) for the first time distinguished psychological state of job involvement from two other psychological states of the worker. They suggest that job involvement refers to the degree to which a person's total work situation is an important part of his life. The job involved person is one who is affected very much personally by his whole job situation, presumably because he perceives his job as an important part of his self- concept and perhaps as a place to satisfy his important needs (e.g. his need for self-esteem).

In review of the psychological literature of job involvement, Saleh and Hosek (1976) identified four different interpretations of concept of Job Involvement. A person is job involved (1) when work to him is of central life interest; (2) when he actively participates in his work; (3) when he perceives performance as central to his self- esteem and (4) when he perceives performance as consistent with his self- concept. The main idea underlying this interpretation is that the psychological state of involvement with respect to an environmental entity is a cognitive or perceived state of identification with that entity. The second interpretation of involvement in terms of participation suggests that the psychological state of involvement be viewed as behavioural acts of the individual directed towards the satisfaction of his or her needs for autonomy and control.

Saleh and Hosek (1976) stated that job involvement is the degree to which a person identifies with the job, actively participates in it and considers his performance important to his self- worth.

Patchen (1970) identified three general conditions for job involvement. According to him, "Where people are highly motivated, where they feel sense of solidarity with the enterprise and where they get a sense of pride for their work, we may speak of them as highly involved in their job." When Patchen talks of workers being highly motivated, he refers to their high levels of achievement need or their wish to accomplish worthwhile things on the job. When he talks of workers' solidarity with the enterprise, he refers to their need for belongingness to the organization. Finally when he talks of workers' sense of pride, he refers to workers' feeling of high self esteem. Thus in Patchen's view, when a job provides opportunities for the satisfaction of one's achievement need belonging need and self esteem need, one experiences a great degree of job involvement.

Originating from the job involvement, intellectual commitment may be defined as an intense and persevering involvement with the intellectual activities. Hummel Rossi (1976) defined intellectual commitment as "an intended and persevering involvement with intellectualism, which is manifested by the active pursuing and preference for intellectual activities." An intellectually committed student is one who prefers intellectual activities (reading a book) to non- intellectual activities (playing football or gossiping) and spends more time on the intellectual activities. A person is intellectually committed when pursuance of intellectual activities to him is of central life interest, when he actively participates in intellectual pursuits and when he considers participation in intellectual activities as central to his self-esteem. Thus intellectual commitment refers to active involvement of the students with intellectual activities for the satisfaction of their achievement need and when they consider participation in intellectual activities important for their self-worth.

Cognitive Variables

The word 'cognitive' pertains to cognition, or to the action or process of knowing; having the attributes of cognizing. In the Encyclopaedia of Psychology, the word cognition has been given the following meanings;

(i) cognition is an expression for every process by which a living creature obtains knowledge of some object or becomes aware of his environment. Cognition processes are perception, discovery, recognition, imagining, judging, memorizing, learning, thinking and often speech;

(ii) cognition is a process of knowing as distinct from volitional or emotional processess;

(iii) cognition refers to a human activity which is intellectual and communicable.

Thus cognitive variables refer to intellectual abilities and include intelligence, problem solving, imagination, concept formation, creativity, reasoning, and academic achievement etc.

In the present study, intelligence and academic achievement were treated as cognitive variables.

Intelligence

Intelligence, the dictionary says, is "the capacity to acquire and apply knowledge." Generally speaking, 'alertness with regard to actual situations of life is an index of Intelligence.'

A variety of definitions have been given by psychologists but the most commonly accepted are as such:

According to Weschler (1958), "Intelligence is the aggregate or the global capacity of the individual to act purposefully, to think rationally and to deal effectively with the environment."

According to Stoddard (1943), "Intelligence is the ability to undertake activities that are characterized by (i) difficulty (2) complexity (3) abstraction (4) economy (5) adaptiveness to goal, (6) social values, and (7) the emergence of originals, and to maintain such activities under conditions that demand a concentration of energy and a resistance to emotional forces.

It is apparent from the definitions that intelligence is not a single or simple faculty, but it includes all the mental abilities like abstract thinking, ability to form possible relations, logical thinking, ability to put things in order, reasoning and ability to solve mathematical problems as are measured by the tests of general mental ability.

Academic Achievement

By achievement we mean proficiency of performance generally measured by standardised task or test, the act of attaining an end or of carrying out a purpose.

Achievement is most commonly applied to performance in educational tests rather than psychological tests, that is, it implies demonstration of acquired ability, skill, knowledge or understanding than inherent capacity.

Academic achievement refers to the degree or level of success or proficiency, attained in some specific area concerning scholastic or academic work. It may have pervasive effect on a student's personal behaviour toward a goal.

In short, academic achievement means knowledge, understanding or skills, acquired after instructions and training in courses or subjects of study. It is generally measured by means of total marks of the students obtained by them in a particular examination.

Non-Cognitive Variables

Non- cognitive variables pertain to non- intellectual factors. These include personality attributes, adjustment, emotional stability, self-concept, socio-economic status etc.

In the present investigation, extraversion- introversion and socio-economic status were probed among non- cognitive variables.

Extraversion- Introversion

Extraversion- introversion are ways of orienting oneself to the world by objects, values and experiences. Jung believed that the normal mind is expressed during either serious tension or irrational thinking. When one or the other modalities predominate, the individual is said to be either a thinking type or an emotional type and these two types are said to be extroverted or introverted.

Extroverted Type. When a person's orientation is determined primarily by objective conditions or facts, he is said to be extroverted. When there is cautious interposition of delayed response between the individual and objective world, the person so oriented is said to be introverted. If a man thinks, feels and acts so that his whole mode of living corresponds directly with objective conditions, he is extroverted. His consciousness, his thinking, his whole subjective life are largely determined by objective factors. His innerself is controlled by external conditions. He believes in immediate environment and his attention and interest are directed almost solely by conditions outside himself. He is interested in persons and things. Accordingly, his actions are determined by them rather than by ideas or abstractions. In his moral life, the extrovert displays the same objective orientation. His moral actions correspond with society's expectations. Accordingly, the extrovert is largely conventional, he behaves as he is expected to behave and not ordinarily inclined to transcend or rebel against the society. Although the extrovert may thus be socially adjusted, he tends to close his eyes to his subjective needs. The behaviour of extrovert is so strongly outward, that he tends to neglect both his body and mind. Continued adjustment to objective conditions hinders subjective impulses from becoming conscious.

Introverted Type

An introvert is motivated predominantly by subjective factors. Although he is not blind to objective conditions, he assimilates them in a more personal manner than the extrovert. In contrast to the extrovert, the introvert finds the inner world of thought, feeling, sensation and intuition most appealing and convincing. In extreme form, bordering on neurosis, the introvert recoils from the external world and protects himself from it by a variety of defence mechanisms which will preserve for him his sense of aloneness in the face of stark reality.

In general, extrovert people are social, open, frank, outgoing, eager to do things, adaptable, not easily worried and embarrased and willing to work with others. The introvert, on the other hand, is normally a contemplative individual who enjoys solitude and satisfaction of quiet life. He is generally shy, self- conscious, gets easily upset, fond of reading, reserved, and inclined to be radical.

Socio- economic status

It is difficult to define the term socio- economic status. The status is a position of a person in the community to which he belongs. A person socially sound may be economically poor while reverse may also be there.

Chaplin (1928) defined socio-economic status "as the position that an individual or family occupies with reference to the prevailing average standards of cultural possessions, effective income and participation in group activity of community."

According to Lovinger (1940) "socio- economic status contains such factors as size of family, race, locality of residence, education of parents, income and occupation."

Rotham (1954) has described socio- economic status "as economic position and prestige, a way of life and a pattern of values."

English and English (1958) in their Comprehensive Dictionary of psychological and Psychoanalytical terms defined socio-economic status as "an individual's position in a given society, as determined by wealth, occupation and social class."

Good (1959), in his dictionary defines socio-economic status as "the level indicative of both, the social and economic achievement of an individual or a group."

The term socio-economic status has been broadly defined by Rangaswamy (1969) to include "educational, professional or occupational and economic status of parents. It also includes the environmetnal facilities available for the individuals."

Biswas and Aggarwal (1971) define 'socio-economic' as "referring to social and economic factors and conditions," and 'status' as "the rank or the position accorded formally to a person within the social strucure of a group."

According to Kuppuswami (1974), the estimation of SES is based on three assumptions; (i) that there is a class structure in society (ii) that status positions are determined mainly by a few commonly accepted symbolic characteristics and (iii) that these characteristics can be scaled and combined using statistical procedures.

Hawes and Hawes (1982) state that socio-economic status is "the background or standing of one or more persons in the society on the basis both of social class and financial situation."

Objectives of the Study

The following were the objectives of the study :

- To construct and standarise an educational interest inventory.
- To study the nature of distribution of scores of seven areas of educational interest and intellectual commitment.
- To study the educational interest patterns of the students belonging to the following groups : (i) sex (ii) different zones (iii) parental qualification (iv) extraversion- introversion ((v) levels of intellectual commitment (vi) levels of academic achievement (vii) levels of intelligence and (vii) levels of socio- economic status.
- To study significance of means difference in different areas of educational interest in relation to the main and interaction effects of the following variables:

(i) sex, (ii) zones (iii) types of school (iv) levels of parental qualification (v) extraversion- introversion (vi) intellectual commitment (vii) academic achievement (viii) intelligence and (ix) socio-economic status.

- To study significance of means difference in the intellectual commitment scores in relation to main and interaction effect of the following variables :

(i) sex (ii) zones (iii) types of school (iv) parental qualification (v) intelligence (vi) socio- economic status.

- To study the significance of means difference in the intellectual commitment scores of (i) high achievers - low achievers and (ii) boys and girls on controlling the influence of intelligence.
- To find out the degree of relationship of each of the seven areas of educational interest with subject-wise and total academic achievement of high school students.

- To find out the co- efficient of co-relation of each of the seven areas of educational interest with socio- economic status, intellectual commitment and intelligence.
- To work out regression- equation for academic achievement of boys and girls when extroversion- introversion, socio- economic status, intellectual commitment, intelligence and adjustment were predictors.

Hypotheses

The following null-hypotheses were tested for the present study in order to achieve the objectives. The hypotheses were tested at .05 level.

- The distribution of educational interest and intellectual commitment scores will not be significantly different from the normal distribution at .05 level.
- There were no significant means difference in the seven areas of educational interest in relation to the main and interaction effects of the following variables ;-

(i) sex (ii) zones (iii) types of school (iv) levels of parental qualification (v) extraversion- introversion (vi) intellectual commitment (vii) academic achievement (viii) intelligence (ix) soci- economic status.

- There were no significant means difference in the intellectual commitment scores in relation to the main and interaction effects of the following variables ;-

(i) Sex (ii) zones (iii) parental qualification (iv) types of school (v) intelligence and (vi) socio- economic status.

- There were no significant means difference in the intellectual commitment scores of high-achievers and low-achievers and (ii) boys and girls on controlling the influence of intelligence.
- There was no relationship of each of the seven areas of

educational interest with the total and subject- wise academic achievement of high school students.

- There was no relationship of each of the seven areas of educational interest with socio- economic status, intellectual commitment and intelligence.
- There was no significant contribution of predictors (introversion, extraversion, socio-economic status, intelligence, intellectual commitment and adjustment) towards the dependent variable (academic achievement).

Operational Definitions Of The Terms

In the present investigation, the investigator used all the concepts as were measured through the psychological tests employed for the collection of information (data) in relation to objectives of the study.

Educational Interest. Educational interest was defined as one's pattern of preferences, likes and dislikes for subjects / activities included in the seven interest areas of educational interest inventory.

Intellectual Commitment. Intellectual commitment meant the active involvement of the students in the academic activities as measured by the intellectual commitment questionnaire.

Intelligence. Intelligence was taken as the ability to solve such items as synonyms, antonyms, number series, classifications, appropriate answer, reasoning and anologies, included in the Jalota's Group Test of General Mental Ability.

Extraversion- Introversion. Extraversion was defined as the tendency to be outgoing and social and introversion was defined as the tendency to be reserved, shy and self- conscious as measured by the extraversion - introversion scale.

Socio- economic status. Socio-economic status was defined as the social, cultural and economic status of the family to which a student belonged. Economic status meant income and material possessions of the family and social status meant the education of the family and occupation of parents. Cultural status of the family referred to the expenditure on newspapers and magazines and concept of social prestige.

Academic Achievement. Academic achievement meant the subject- wise and aggregate marks obtained by the students in their high school examination. The marks of the students were taken in the form of percentage.

Delimitations of the Study

Keeping in view the limited time and facilities at disposal of the researcher, the present study was delimited to the area and scope of the population as well as the content of the study. The study was delimited in the following manner :

- The study was conducted on 10th class students studying in high and higher secondary schools.
- The study was confined to a final sample of 500 students.
- The intelligence and academic achievement were only taken among the cognitive variables.
- The extroversion- introversion, socio- economic status and adjustment were only taken as non- cognitive variables.
- The educational interest inventory was constructed taking into account only seven areas.
- The study was confined to urban sample only.
- The translated questionnaire of intellectual commitment was used.
- Caste- wise treatment of different variables could not be done.
- Hindi speaking students were only included in the sample.
- The study was confined to Jammu division only.

2

Related Studies: An Overview

Research takes the advantage of the knowledge which has been accumulated in the past as a result of constant human endeavour. The researches which have been carried out earlier are an essential aspect of investigation. It is obviously imprudent and wasteful groping in the dark without reviewing what has been done before.

The present chapter aims at giving a brief review of the researches done in the area related to the present investigation. The purpose of reviewing the earlier researches is not only to economise the historical perspective of the present work but also to take cognizance of related studies which employed one or more variables included in this study. Review of previous studies related with the present study served the following specific purposes:

- It enabled the investigator to develop an overall idea about the nature and findings of the previous studies and to arrive at a rationale for the present study.
- It highlighted the methods, procedures and instruments adopted in the previous studies.
- It helped in identifying the gaps in the researches conducted in the chosen field and to explore the facts which had remained unexplored in the previous studies.
- The findings of the earlier studies were utilized to substantiate and support, wherever necessary, the interpretation of the results of the present study.

The studies on interest were classified into two broad categories (a) Studies Abroad (b) Studies in India. The studies were further classified into the following areas : (i) Interest Patterns (ii) Interest and Intelligence (iii) Interest and Socio- Economic Status (iv) Interest and Academic Achievement (v) Interest and miscellaneous Variables.

Studies Abroad

Interest Patterns

Jersild and Tasch (1949) in their study of high school children titled 'Children's Interests and What They Suggest for Education' found that at the high school stage the adolescent boys showed an increased interest in crafts and mechanical arts whereas girls showed increased interest in aesthetic and literary subjects.

Rothney (1937) investigated into the interests of public secondary school boys and the study revealed a wide dispersion of likes among division of interests. Science was equally popular among boys and girls whereas commerce was pet subject of boys only. Surprisingly enough, some male students showed their liking for household course, and a few female students showed their preference for masculine subjects like agriculture.

Jackson (1953) in his investigation found that english, mathematics and science were reported most valuable and social studies least valuable in the area of work.

A number of investigations had been carried out to ascertain the interest patterns on the basis of gender. Studies made by Terman and Miles (1936), Carter and Strong (1933) Yum (1942), Strong (1943), Kuder (1939), Traxler and Mecall (1941) and Jersild and Tasch (1949) all agreed that men tend to be more interested in physical activity, mechanical and scientific matters, politics and selling etc. Interest in art, music, literature, teaching and social work were more characteristic of women.

Delano, Omobolade (1995) used both quantitative and qualitative methodologies to investigate 240 male and female students at the secondary school grade level in South Western region of Nigeria for the factors that influence educational aspirations of Yoruba youth in Nigeria. 119 (49.6%) were females and 121 (50.40%) were males. The purpose of the study was to identify gender differences in the educational goals of the population studied as measurd by enrolment size and educational aspirations.

Data analysis showed that gender disparities existed in the enrolment size of sedondary school students. Evidence of differences in educational aspirations of males and females existed in the population studied. Aspirations to traditional male fields such as engineering, computer science, science and military were unpopular among the females. Aspirations to traditional female professions, such as, nursing and home management were among females. Socio-economic status of the parents had significant impact on the educational aspiration of the females. Educational aspirations of the females from high SES backgrounds significantly differed from educational aspirations of females from low socio-economic status. The higher the SES of the femaels, the more likely they were showing aspirations towards traditional male professions. Male students, regardless of their socio-economic background maintained their affinity to traditional male professions.

Studies Related to General/Educational/Vocational Interest and Intelligence

The pioneer investigations on interest were made by Thorndike (1917). He conducted a study on 'Early interests, their Permanence and Relation to Abilities.' He asked first one hundred and afterwards three hundred forty four college students to rank seven general educational subjects in order of their interests. At the same time the students were asked to rank these educational subjects according to their abilities in them. The study reported the correlation between the individual's rank of abilities and his rank of interests in school subjects.

Reed (1940) used the Henmon Nelson Test of Mental Ability

and Thurstone Vocational Interest Inventory to study the relationship between vocational interest and intelligence. He reported low correlations which were statistically insignificant.

Alteneder (1940) in his study on 'The Value of Intelligence, Personality and Vocational Interest Tests in a Guidance Programme' obtained positive correlations between some of the occupational interests and intelligence but correlations were not statistically significant.

Berdie (1945) undertook a study to see what relationship existed between the total number of 'likes' reported by an individual and his intelligence. He found no significant relationship between them.

Tyler (1951) designed a study to determine the relationship of interests to abilities among first grade children. He obtained significant relationships between the interest in 'Paper Activities' and mental ability in general for boys.

Burt (1962) in his study of relationship between intelligence and attainment found out that the multiple correlation of intelligence and interest with achievement gave a high value of correlations. The value of Pearson's rs for different values was ranging from 0.43 to 0.69.

Interest and Academic Achievement

McClelland (1942) made an investigation into the performance of school subjects of a group of 227 people of the qualifying stage in a Scottish Industrial Centre. A five point scale was used while the pupils were given a list of 16 school subjects and asked to express their interest in each. The aim of the study was to explore the possible use of the interest test in selection for secondary school education. It was found that the correlation coefficient between the interests and attainments given by the pupils was 0.95.

Burt (1962) in his study of relationship between intelligence and attainment found that multiple correlation of intelligence and interest with achievement gave a high value of correlations. The value of Pearson's rs for different values was ranging from 0.43 to 0.69.

Townsend (1945) in his study of 'Achievement and Interest Rating for High School Boys' found a slight positive correlation between achievement and interest which was not statistically significant.

Interest and Socio-economic Status

Gustad (1954) designed a study titled 'Vocational Interests and Socio-Economic Status' to know whether various interest groups differed in terms of socio-economic status and also to find out the relationship among various status measures. He found no significant correlation among the three status measures studied. Only the occupational level differentiated significantly among interest groups.

Renee, P. (1994) made an investigation on 'African eighth graders: Factors affecting their educational and occupational aspirations. The study used cross-sectional data from the National Education longitudinal study of eighth graders to examine five domains of influence on the educational and occupational aspirations of 2,607 African American eight graders. The five domains were familial, school, teacher and neighbourhood measures. In addition, placement in ability groups and access to social resources were included in the analysis as mediating factors. The regression analysis showed that the most important predictions of aspirations were grades, poverty status, parents expectations and attending a Catholic school. Reading test scores, father's occupation, parent's education, low-ability group assignment in two courses, and discussing high school plans and careers with a teacher and an adult outside of the family also tended to be important for educational aspirations while gender, attending school in rural areas and high ability group assignment in one or two courses were important for occupational aspirations.

Studies in India

Interest Patterns

Rangaswami (1958) conducted an investigation into the interests of high school pupils in Mysore state. He studied their interests in (i) newspaper (ii) co-curricular activities (iii) hobbies, (iv) library and (v) school subjects and concluded that a very large number of pupils expressed great liking for literacy subjects, mathematics, science subjects such as physics, chemistry and biology. Commerce was liked very much by the urban pupils, whereas rural boys expressed liking for agriculture as school subject.

Sharma (1956) investigated the curricular and co-curricular interests of adolescent girls of Delhi and found that the interest patterns of girls were different from those of adolescent boys.

Arora (1955) studied the vocational and co-curricular activities of adolescents of Delhi. He found liking of students for science, constructive and aesthetic activities. Some students also showed their liking to study domestic science as a subject at high school level.

Singh (1959) in his investigation, studied the interests patterns of high school and higher secondary school adolescents of Rajasthan. He found that the occupation interests of urban and rural adolescents differed significantly in aesthetic, literary and agriculture areas.

Verma (1965) in his research paper 'On the Career of Girls' showed that the changing values in India had made the Indian females vocationally minded and they were prepared to work in a number of vocations like literary, scientific, commercial, crafts, aesthetic, social services and outdoor etc. Surprisingly enough, he found that the girls also showed some interest for agricultural vocation. The rural girls were interested in household, social service, literary and scientific vocations more than the urban girls whereas later were interested in agricultural, aesthetic and creative vocations more than the former.

Pandey (1960) in his Project 'our Adolescents, theri Interests and Education' studied the (i) personal interests, (ii) social interests (3) recreational interests (4) sex interests (5) school work interests and (6) vocational interests of adolescents of U.P. He found that rural adolescents in order of preference liked science, hindi, civics, english, economics, mathematics, geography, agriculture, commerce, art and history and the urban adolescents in order of their preference liked science, hindi, english, commerce, agriculture, geography, mathematics, economics, sanskrit, civics, art, and history. Science was considered most valuable subject by the adolescents. Commerce was considered to be of greater importance by the urban adolescents than the rural ones. Agriculture was considered more valuable by the rural boys.

Patel (1967) made a critical study of recreational, socio-cultural, intellectual and occupational interests of high school pupils in Gujrat and tried to find out differences in interests, if any, due to age, sex, rural-urban region and cultural areas. The sample consisted of 3, 963 pupils of classes IX, X and XI , both boys and girls in the age group of 13 + to 15+ drawn from schools of nine districts of Gujrat belonging to twelve different cultural regions. The data was collected by using a questionnaire. It was found that travel and sports activities received first and second preferences among recreational interests. In socio-cultural interests, pupils' responses indicated two items very prominently, namely collection of funds for charity shows and organizing students' council. Among the intellectual activities, class debates, general debates and book reading received preferences. The profession of medicine and engineering had the maximum appeal, while clerical work the minimum. On a comparative analysis it was found that the differences in interests on the basis of age and sex were significant. The differences on the basis of districts, urban, semi-urban and rural were significant in a few cases.

Singh (1967) investigated into the patterns of educational and vocational interests of adolescents. The purpose of the investigation was to test the hypothesis regarding the differences in the interests on account of sex and rural-urban origin and the relationship between the educational interests, the vocational interests and courses of study. The entire student population of urban and rural higher secondary schools and intermediate colleges of Agra district was stratified into four groups- urban male students, urban female students, rural male students and rural female students. A group of 500 students consisting of 125 urban boys, 125 urban girls, 125 rural girls and 125 rural boys were drawn. For measuring educational and vocational interests, an educational and a vocational interest inventory were prepared. The findings revealed that the educational and vocational interests of adolescents were not in agreement and their educational courses of subjects for study and vocational interests were not directly related. The high school students were studying courses which they did not like and which seemed not to be in line with their vocational preferences. Significant sex and rural-urban differences were also found in educational and vocational likings.

Singh (1972) conducted a study of the interest Patterns of school- going boys and girls and their educational implications. The study was conducted on a sample of 720 boys and 360 girls, selected through a stratified random sampling technique, from the institutions (six for boys and four for girls) of four districts. The variables considered in the study were sex and grade. The seventh, ninth and eleventh grade students were taken up. The tools used were the observation, interview with children and with their parents .The data thus collected were treated with product moment correlation technique. The centroid method was used for factorisation to study the nature of clusters. The study found (i) the boys interested in sports, games, scientific, constructive and productive activities, (ii) the age of ninth class was peak age for the expression of interests. This was the crucial age for both the sexes. Aesthetic area, altruistic area, personal aspect, acquisitive instinct area were highly preferred among girls (iii) the play area was nearly common area for both the sexes and (iv) curiosity area, social activity and community life were more liked areas among boys in comparison to girls.

Samal (1977) made an investigation to have a differential study of the interest patterns of high school seniors (sex-wise and place-wise). The study was undertaken on a stratified, random sample of 570 boys and 580 girls of tenth class of the recognized high schools of Orissa. The vocational interest inventory developed for the purpose was an interactive free response variety of self-reporting instrument giving measures on eight scales of vocational interest, namely, scientific, mechanical, agriculture, business, social service, arts, clerical and administrative. The odd-even reliability of the interest scales ranged from 0.79 to 0.93. Inter-correlations among the scales varied from –0.06 to 0.31. The instrument was validated against the California Interest Inventory. Sex-wise difference was found significant in administrative, business, social service and arts scales of interest. Placewise stratification had no impact on variation of interest scores. The sample displayed a very high degree of interest in social service, agriculture and science.

Zargar and Matoo (1993) conducted a study on 'creative thinking ability and vocational interests.' The objective was to assess and compare the vocational interests (fine-arts and literary) of high and low creative students.The sample for the study consisted of one thousand 10th class students (700 boys and 300 girls) randomly drawn from 26 govt. secondary schools of Anantnag district (J&K). The data was collectd by administering Mehdi's Verbal Test of Creative Thinking and Chatterji's Non-Language Preference Record. Identification of high and low creative categories was made on the basis of 75th percentile and 25th percentile respectively. Two way analysis of variance was used to find out the significant differences between high and low creative categories. The results revealed that the two groups differed on their vocational interests. High creatives showed tendency towards fine arts and literary interests. Further sex as a variable could not make any significant difference in the interest pattern of high and low creatives.

Panda (1994) conducted a study to find out the vocational interests and academic performance of tribal adolescents. The sample of the study consisted of 200 tribal adolescents (100 male and 100 female) studying in class X of two tribal districts of Arunachal Pradesh. They were selected randomly from six higher secondary schools and the sample was matched with age and residential background. The subjects were adminsitered vocational interest record (Kulshreshtha, 1984) which measures ten independent dimensions of vocational interests namely literary, scientific, executive, commercial, constructive, artistic, agriculture, persuasive, social and household. 't' test was used to analyse the data. The resutls revealed that there was a significant difference between males and females in vocational interests and no significant difference in academic performance. The tribal male adolescents seemed to have more inclination towards vocation of executive or administrative (Rank-I), followed by social service (Rank-2), Scientific (Rank-3) and least interest in the vocation of commercial (Rank-10). The female students showed more preference to the vocation of household (Rank-1), followed by artistic (Rank-2), executive (Rank-3) and least interest in the vocation of constructive (Rank-10).

Interest and Intelligence

Rastogi (1965) conducted a study of 'Interests, Intelligence and Achievement in High School Students' and found a coefficient of correlation between interest and I.Q.0.31.

Samal, S. (1970) undertook a study to investigate the relationship of interest with intelligence. The study was undertaken on a stratified random sample of 570 boys and 580 girls, of tenth class of the recognized schools of Orissa. The vocational interest inventory developed for the purpose was an interactive free response variety of self-reporting instrument giving measures on eight scales of vocational interest, namely scientific, mechanical, agriculture, business, social service, arts, clerical and administrative. The odd-even reliability of the interest scales ranged from 0.79 to 0.93. The instrument was validated against the California Interest Inventory. The CFIT scale 3 was used to measure the subjects' intelligence. Correlation between vocational interest and other variables was computed by the product moment method. It was found that none of the interest scales correlated significantly with intelligence and there was no marked difference in interest of high and low intelligence groups.

Devi and Basavana (1985) in their study of interests in relation to intelligence among women college students found that individuals with high intelligence scores expressed interests in physical and biological sciences while students with low intelligence scores were interested in linguistic, humanities, art, and music areas.

Interest and Academic Achievement

Dutt (1952) investigated into the relationship between interest and achievement in arithmetic and found high significant correlation between the interest and achievement in arithmetic.

Rastogi (1968) conducted a study to find out relationship between interest and achievement in high school students. He found positive correlation between interest and achievement in science with coefficient of correlation 0.37.

Vishnoi (1977) studied the interest patterns of high and low achievers. The sample consisted of one hundred eighty four eleventh class male students (arts group) belonging to different intermediate colleges located within the jurisdiction of a Allahabad Municipal Corporation. The high and low achievers were classified on the basis of examination marks, i.e., total marks of the High School Examination Those who scored 60 percent or above were grouped as high achievers, while those who scored between 33 percent and 44 percent were grouped as low achievers. Chatterjee's Non- language Preference Record was used for measuring the interest of the subjects. It was found that high achievers were more interested in science and craft activities than low achievers. Low achievers were more interested in agricultural and household activities. Both the groups showed an almost equal interest in the areas of fine arts, literature, technical, outdoor and sports activities. Academic achievement in both the groups was not found to have any substantial relationship with the areas of interest except literary activities with respect to high achievers and agricultural activities with respect to low achievers.

Interest and Socio-Economic Status

Bhatia (1962) conducted a study of relationship between vocational preferences, socio-economic status and curricular choice of students of class XI of Delhi schools. He found that there was some relationship between vocational preferences and parents' occupations. The students belonging to the highest income group had expressed comparatively more preferences for the scientific area. The students belonging to the lowest income group had expressed comparatively more preference for the clerical area.

Samal (1977) undertook an investigation to study the relationship of interest with socio-economic status. One of the objectives of Samal's study was to find out the relationship between vocational interest and socio-economic status. The study was undertaken on a stratified, random sample of 570 boys and 580 girls of tenth class of the recognized high schools of Orissa. The vocational interest inventory developed for the purpose was an interactive free response variety of self- reporting instrument namely, scientific, mechanical, agriculture, business, social service, arts, clerical and administrative. Assuming that education, occupation and income are the potential contributors of one's socio-economic status, a scale was devised to measure this variable. Inter correlations among three aspects of scale ranged from 0.36 to 0.62. Correlation between vocational interest and socio- economic status was computed by the product moment method. Interest in agriculture, business and clerical activities correlated negatively with socio-economic status.

Pathak (1978) studied the effect of family background on the development of interests. He found that low income group scored low on outdoor, mechanical and scientific areas of interest.

Joshi (1983) made an investigation into the interests of higher secondary school going pupils. One of the objectives of the study was to study the differences in the interests of these students in relation to their parents' education and socio-economic status. The interest inventory constructed and standardised by Parikh, socio-economic status scale constructed and standardised by Kuppuswamy for urban areas and socio-economic status scale constructed and standardised by Pareek and Trivedi for rural areas was used for data collection. The data was collected from a sample of 1000 students selected at random. A factorial design and analysis of variance was used for drawing conclusions. The pupils of higher socio-economic status group were more interested in the administrative, natural, outdoor, scientific and fine arts topics than those of low socio-economic status group.

Yadav (2000) conducted a study of relationship between socio-economic status and vocational preferences of adolescents in the Ahirwal region of Haryana. The objectives of the study were to find out the extent to which socio-economic status acts as a motive for the vocational preferences of adolescents. The sample comprised 240 students each from three streams i.e., science, arts and commerce, studying in XI class in eight different colleges of rural and urban areas of Ahirwal region of Haryana. Thurstone's vocational interest schedule, socio-economic status scale (rural and urban) by S.P. Kulshretha were employed for data collection. The collected data was analysed usign the coefficient of correlation. The study revealed that most of the students preferred executive work and showed least interest in the area of artistic work and music. Urban students gave their preference for the jobs related to the field of physical sciences whereas rural students preferred the field of executive work. Science students preferred the field of physical and biological sciences whereas art students were found interested in the field of executive work and commerce students gave their preference for the field of linguistics and computational work. Socio-economic status was found to play a significant role in the selection of vocational preferences. Students belonging to the higher socio-economic status gave preference to executive work, computational work and physical sciences, students belonging to the middle socio-economic status gave greater preference to the field of executive work, physical science and biological sciences and students of low socio-economic status gave preference to the field of physical and biological sciences. Urban students gave preference to business whereas rural students showed more interest in service.

Hmingthanzala (2001) made an investigation into the vocational interest and occupational aspirations of class-X students of district headquarters of Mizoram as related to socio-economic status and academic achievement. The objectives of the study were to obtain information about the types of interest of high school students of Mizoram (ii) to differentiate between the vocational interests and occupational aspirations of students from different types of school and (v) to find out the relationship between the occupational aspirations and vocational interests of the students. Twenty-five percent of the secondary school students selected using multi-staged stratified random sampling technique from schools of district headquarters of Mizoram like Aizawal, Lunglei and Saiha Served as a sample for the study. The tools used for data collection were Interest Record (Singh, 1960), Occupational Aspiration Scale (Guwal, 1975), Socio-economic Status scale (Srivastva, 1991) and Academic Achievement scores from class examination conducted by MBSE, Aizawal. Pearson's Product Moment coefficient of correlation and CR were used to analyse the data. The findings revealed that boys were having significantly higher interest in mechanical and outdoor areas whereas girls had higher interest is business, aesthetic and clerical areas. A significant difference was observed between the students of different districts. Students belonging to high socio-economic status were having significantly higher interest in outdoor area. It was found that there was significantly negative correlation between interest factor in mechanical area and Mizo and English language. The students who had higher innterest in business were found good in english, social science and overall academic achievement. It was found that the students having scientific and social interest had high occupational aspirations whereas students having high interest in business, aesthetic and outdoor areas did not have high occupational aspirations. Students from high socio-economic status families had high occupational aspirations and vice-versa. There was no significant relation between subject and their interest in mechanical and outdoor activities and age of the student and occupational aspirations.

The review of related literature reveals that in all the research studies in India and abroad, the most of the work has been done in the area of measuring general or vocational Interests Studies which have been conducted to measure likings for various school subjects were very less in number. Very few studies have been conducted to ascertain the relationship between interest, intelligence and academic achievement. Hardly any macro study is available exclusively on educational interest patterns and to study intellectual commitment and educational interest in relation to socio-economic status, intelligence, academic achievement, adjustment and introversion- extraversion. Therefore, the study "Intellectual Commitment and Educational Interest in Relation to Certain Cognitive and Non-Cognitive Variables" was an attempt towards filling up gap in the field of educational research.

3

The Present Study

Introduction

After the problem of research has been stated and objectives have been fixed and hypotheses for investigation have been formed, it is necessary to develop a suitable research design for testing the hypotheses. Research design is a plan of action, a plan for collecting and analysing the data. The selection of an appropriate research design is very essential because it has the following two basic purposes: (i) to provide answers to research questions as validly, objectively, accurately and economically as possible (2) to control the experimental, extraneous and error variances of the particular research problem under study.

The research designs range from the simple design to factorial design. No design is the best. The most important criterion is that the design should be appropriate for testing particular hypotheses of the study. For achieving the objectives and testing the hypotheses, the investigator adopted a combination of descriptive research method (survey and correlational design) and experimental research method(factorial design). The relevant detail about the plan and procedure is given in the following steps:

- Population.
- Selection of the sample.
- The tools used
- Scoring procedure

- Statistical techniques used
- Tabulation and organization of data.

Population

A 'population' may refer to all of any specified groups of human beings or of characteristics of human beings, or of non human entities such as objects, geographical areas, time units, events, methods, schools, or even the behaviour of inanimate objects, such as, the throw of dice or the tossing of a coin. The population in the present study was students (boys and girls) of 15 years age who were studying in x class in high and higher secondary schools of Jammu province.

The sample

A 'Sample' is a miniature representation of and selected from a larger group or aggregate. In other words, the sample provides a specimen picture of a larger whole. It is not possible to include all units of a population in a study in order to arrive at valid conclusion. Moreover, the sizes of populations are often so large that the study of all the units would not only be expensive but also cumbersome and time consuming. Reasearch, therefore, is invariably conducted by means of a sample drawn from the population through some sampling technique, on the basis of which generalizations are arrived at and made applicable to the target population.

The sampling for the present investigation was done in three stages. (i) the pilot work (ii) try out and (iii) final. The samples for the pilot work and try out have been discussed in the later section of this chapter under the heading 'Construction of Educational Interest Inventory'. Therefore, the sample selected for the collection of final data is only discussed here.

Sample for the collection of final data

The final draft of educational interest inventory along with other tests was administered to a stratified random sample of 500 students of 15 years age group studying in government and private schools of Jammu province. There are six districts in Jammu province. But the study was restricted to five districts only because the sixth district is far off from the other districts and its academic session is also different. Each district was taken a unit to form a different strata. The sampling for the districts was further confined to district headquarter level only because some of the tests were workable only on urban population. One hundred subjects were to be taken from each district headquarter. The investigator ascertained the number of schools in each district headquarter and selected two schools from each district headquarter, one for the boys and another for the girls. The private schools were selected only from the Jammu district. The sample of 50 boys and 50 girls was randomly chosen from the 10th class of each selected school. This way, a total sample of 500 was chosen from the five districts of jammu province namely Jammu, Udhampur, Kathua, Poonch and Rajouri. The list of the institutions along with the respective number of students chosen from each institution is presented in the Table 3.1.

The Tools used

In every type of research, the investigator needs certain devices to gather facts and explore new fields. The devices thus employed as means to collect data are called tools. Different tools are available for measuring varied traits for various purposes. The researcher has to select from the available tools which will provide data for testing hypothesis. In selecting tests for collecting data, researcher must evaluate their reliability, validity and useability. Further, various other considerations such as personal competence of the research to administer, score and interpret the test results also affect the selection of tests. Since the purpose of the present investigation was to study the intellectual commitment and educational interest patterns of high school students in relation to their certain cognitive and non-cognitive variables, the following tools were used.

Table 3.1: School-Wise Distribution of the Students Selected for the Collection of Final Data

S.No.	*Name of the Institution*	*No. of students taken*	
		Boys	*Girls*
1.	Govt. Girls Higher Secondary School Poonch	—	50
2.	Govt. Boys Higher Secondary School Poonch	50	—
3.	Govt Girls Higher Secondary School Rajouri	—	50
4.	Govt. Boys Higher Secondary School Rajouri	—	50
5.	Govt. Girls Higher Secondary School Kathua	50	—
6.	Govt. Boys Higher Secondary School Kathua	—	50
7.	Govt. M.L.H.S. School Udhampur	50	—
8.	Govt. Girls High School Udhampur	—	50
9.	Jagriti Niketan Jammu	25	25
10.	Luthra Academy Jammu	25	25
	Total	*250*	*250*

- Educational Interest Inventory (constructed and standardised by the investigator)
- Intellectual Commitment Scale (developed by Chitra Srinivas and translated into hindi by the investigator).
- Jalota's Group Test of General Mental Ability.
- Saxena's Adjustment Inventory.
- Personality Inventory (Extroversion - Introversion) Scale by Singh and Singh.

- Socio-Economic Status Scale (developed by Jalota, Pandey, Kapoor and Singh and modified by the investigator).

The tools are briefly described hereafter.

Educational Interest Inventory (Constructed and Standardised by the Investigator)

The investigator constructed an educational interest inventory on the pattern of Strong Vocational Interest Blank. The investigator had to think about the possible areas of educational interest. For this literature was studied, discussions were held and varied interest patterns related with different streams of education were derived.

Pilot work. The investigator could not pick up the interest areas arbitrarily. The pilot work was done for this purpose. A list of number of areas namely agriculture, fine arts, constructive, productive, recreational, mechanical, humanities, literary, business, commercial, home-science, aesthetic, science and technology was prepared and administered to one hundred subjects for showing their preferences. The subjects were in two groups; one group comprising 50 teachers and another group comprising 50 students. They were asked to show their preferences to the possible areas of educational interest. The teachers and students had an agreement only on seven interest areas where they gave maximum preferences. The maximum preferences were ascertained through the percentages calculated for each area. Those seven areas as having maximum preferences were finally picked up for the construction of educational interest inventory. The seven selected areas were as:

Agriculture. The agriculture interest area included the subjects and activities like animal husbandry, farming, study of manures, horticulture, dairying, agriculture, extension of rural sociology, agricultural botany, veterinary science etc.

Fine Arts. Fine Arts area of interest was represented by the subjects/ activities like clay modelling, toy making, handicrafts, wood craft, music, drawing, painting, sketching, art of interior decoration and other activities included in the work experience programme.

Commerce . Commerce area covered such subjects and activities like elements of commerce, commercial geography, economics, accountancy, business correspondence, short-hand, typing, banking, shop management, business management and foreign trade.

Humanities. Humanities area of educational interest included subjects like hindi, History, geography, English literature, regional literature, economics, philosophy, sociology, psychology, political science etc.

Home Science. Home science area was covered through the subjects and activities like, general home science, cooking, sewings, cutting, embroidery, knitting, home-management, home decoration and child care etc.

Science. Science area was represented by the subjects like, physics, chemistry, zoology, geology, botany, mathematics, physiology and general science etc.

Technology. Technology field of interest included such subjects and activities like, electrical, mechanical and civil engineering, welding and fitter's job, draftman's job, radio / T.V. engineering, applied mathematics etc.

Response Categories

It was decided to use three category response i.e 'Like' , 'Indifferent' and 'Dislike' on the pattern of Strong's Vocational Interest Blank and Jingran's Interest Inventory.

Construction of Items for the Preliminary Draft

Keeping in view the content of the each area, 50 items were prepared for each area of interest with the total of 350 items for the whole educational interest inventory. Before the try out of the inventory, it was again sent to the teachers and language experts to seek their suggestions for improvement. The ambiguities and inadequacies were checked at this stage and the items were modified accordingly.

Compilation of the Items

In each interest area, the first twenty five items were arranged in 'L.I.D.' sequence whereas last twenty five items were arranged in 'D.I.L.' sequence. This process was followed in order to minimise faked and biased responses. Instructions and examples for the pre-try out were also prepared.

Pre-try out

It has been suggested by the experts in the field of measurement and evaluation that the newly constructed tool should be administered to the small sample of 15 to 20 individuals before the actual 'tryout' so that the major ambiguities and inadequacies in the directions and items may be discovered and the amount of time for the later 'tryout' may be adjusted.

The prepared inventory consisting of 350 items was administered to a group of fifteen students of tenth grade. No time limit was set up but time allowance was adjusted so that at least 90% subjects could attempt all items. The ambiguities and inadequacies as perceived by the examiners were removed at this stage as well and the inventory was set ready for the try out.

Tryout

The following steps were followed at the try out stage:

(a) Sample for the collection of data.

The data for the try out stage was collected through a stratified random sample of 300 students (boys and girls) studying in high and higher secondary schools of the three districts of Jammu province namely Jammu, Udhampur and Kathua. Names of the institutions along with number of students selected at the try out stage are given in the following table:

Table 3.2. School-Wise distribution of the Students Selected at the Try out Stage

S.No.	*Name of the Institution*	*No. of students taken*	
		Boys	*Girls*
1.	Jagriti Niketan Jammu	25	25
2.	Luthra Academy Jammu	25	25
3.	Govt. Girls Higher Secondary School Kathua	—	50
4.	Govt. Boys Higher Secondary School Kathua	50	—
5.	Govt. Girls High School Udhampur	—	50
6.	Govt. M.L.H.S. School Udhampur	50	—
	Total	150	150

Age and Grade of the Students

The x class students of age 15+ were chosen for the try out of the inventory. X class in the ladder of the education is the crucial stage upto which the students get general education of the basic knowledge of all the subjects such as language, science, mathematics, social science and arts etc. After this class, there is a diversification of the courses and the students start thinking about their future career. Moreover, aptitudes and interests take definite shape at this age as the students start attaining maturity and the intelligence is also developed.

Administration of the Inventory

Instructions laid down in the inventory were read out to the subjects before the start of the try out. One student was made to sit on one desk so that the students might not copy from one another.

Though the inventory was untimed, yet it took the students 60 to 70 minutes to complete the inventory.

Scoring Procedure

Responses were scored on 'L.I.D.' Pattern. Two marks were to be given to each liked response, one mark to each indifferent response and zero to the disliked response.

Selection of the items for the Final Draft

The final draft was made up of the items which are most suitable and appropriate for measuring the construct under consideration. In measures of typical performance, homogenous keying is considered most favourable Cronbach (1984), Brown (1976), Mehrens and Lehmann (1973) and Thorndike (1970). That is, the Sine qua non in scale construction is that the scale must be homogenous. Thornlike advocated that homogenous key appears to have clearer validity as a description of the individual (construct validity). When the items are all chosen because of their relationship to one another, there is common theme tying them together, we can describe the person in terms of such constructs as interest in science, interest in agriculture etc. The appropriateness of the items was checked through item discrimination. Two contrast groups of high and low scores were formed through the use of quartiles. The frequencies on each of the items were counted and mean values were calculated against each item for high and low groups. The critical ratio was applied to test significance of means difference. Moreover, inter-item and item-total correlations in each area were got calculated. There were 50 items in each area. The investigator made up 50×50 matrix of each area of interest to give desired number of inter-correlations. It was a very stupendous task for the investigator to compute inter-item and item-total correlations manually. The computer services were utilized for this purpose. The correlations were calculated with the help of contingency co- efficient. Thorndike (1970) and Mehrens (1973) recommended that for an item to be finally selected, it must show a correlation of more than 0.60 with other items and total. Items showing correlation coefficient of more than 0.60 were also got identified from the computer. The investigator got from the computer the serial number of the items which were having inter-item and item-total correlation of more than 0.60. This procedure of selecting the items for the final draft of interest inventory has already been followed in United States by OVIS. The minimum number of items having inter-item correlation coefficient of more than 0.60 and significant value of C.R. was 25 in one of the areas. Hence, 25 items having inter-item and item-total correlation coefficient of 0.60 or more with higher significant C.R were spotted out in each of the seven areas. The final draft of the inventory was made up of 175 items in total. The items selected were randomly arranged. In each interest area, the first thirteen items were arranged in 'L. I.D.' sequence whereas the last twelve items were arranged in 'D.I.L.' sequence. The inventory was got printed for the final administration to find out reliability, validity and to establish norms.

Reliability of the Educational Interest Inventory

The investigator found the test retest and split half reliability coefficients for each of the seven areas of education interest inventory. The sample for ascertaining reliability was comprised one hundred students (boys and girls). In case of test retest method, retesting was done on the same group of students after a gap of 15 to 20 days. For the split half reliability coefficients, each areas was splitted into two halves on the basis of odd-even items. The correlation co-efficients were computed between the two halves of each area. This gave reliability for half the test of each of the seven areas. Spearman's Brown Prophecy formula was applied to get the reliability coefficients for the full length of each of the seven areas.

The reliability coefficients have been given in the table 3.3.

Composite Reliability of the Educational Interest Inventory

As the educational interest inventory was composed of seven areas, the estimation of composite reliability was needed. The reliability of a composite score is a function of the reliabilities of its components, their dispersions, their inter correlations and the respective weights assigned to them. Composite reliability of the inventory was computed by Mosier's (1943) formula.

Table 3.3. Reliability Coefficients for the Seven Areas of Educational Interest Inventory

	Areas	*Test Retest Reliability Coefficients*	*Split halves reliability Coefficients*	*Total Reliability Coefficients*
1.	Agriculture	.88	.72	.83
2.	Fine Arts	.90	.69	.81
3.	Commerce	.92	.74	.85
4.	Humanities	.91	.67	.80
5.	Home Science	.93	.81	.89
6.	Science	.94	.83	.90
7.	Technology	.93	.79	.88

In order to calculate the composite reliability of the seven areas, the standard deviation of each of the seven areas, reliability coefficient of each component and the inter- correlations between seven areas were calculated. These calculated values are shown in table 3.4.

On applying Mosier formula to the values given in table 3.4, the composite reliability was found to be 0.94.

Validity

The concurrent validity of the inventory was found by correlating the scores of the present inventory with Labh Singh's Educational Interest Inventory. A sample of one hundred subjects (boys and girls) was chosen for determining the validity of educational interest inventory. The coefficient of validity came out to be 0.72.

The standardisation of an inventory also involved the setting up of norms which have been presented in chapter IV.

Table 3.4. The Values Substituted in the Mosier Formula

	Areas	*Weight*	*S.D. of the scores of each area*	*Reliability coefficient of each area*	*Inter-correlations*
1.	Agriculture	1	8.29	.83	å$_{12}$ = .98
					å$_{13}$ = .21
					å$_{14}$ = .24
					å$_{15}$ = .14
					å$_{16}$= .06
					å$_{17}$ = .35
2.	Fine Arts	1	9.32	.81	å$_{23}$ = .32
					å$_{24}$ = .50
					å$_{25}$ = .02
					å$_{26}$ = .30
					å$_{27}$ = .52
3.	Commerce	1	9.14	.85	å$_{34}$ = .27
					å$_{35}$ = .09
					å$_{36}$ = .14
					å$_{37}$ = .37
4.	Humanities	1	10.75	.80	å$_{45}$ = .34
					å$_{46}$ = .01
					å$_{47}$ = .29
5.	Home	1	12.88	.89	å$_{56}$ = .47
	Science				å$_{57}$ = .10
6.	Science	1	11.05	.90	å$_{67}$ = .30
7.	Technology	1	11.82	.88	

Intellectual commitment scale

For measuring the intellectual commitment of the students, the investigator translated the English version of intellectual commitment scale developed by Chitra Srinivas into Hindi. It was originally developed by Srinivas on the model of job involvement scale of Lodhal and Kejner (1965) and by including 7 items from the teacher and student study used by Singhal (1977) with a total of 27 items. It was presented for its reliability by giving it to eight raters. The items on which the raters were not able to differentiate on items across categories were dropped. There were eight such items. The remaining 19 items were then again given to eight student raters from Jawaharlal Nehru University.

Out of the 19 items in total, fourteen measure commitment and five measure non-commitment. The items were to be responded on five point scale ranging from 'very true,' 'true,' 'doubtful; 'false' and 'very false'. The maximum score on the scale can be 95. There is no time limit for the scale to be completed, yet it can be completed satisfactorily in ten minutes. It is useful for both boys and girls and can be administered on groups as well as on an individual.

The original scale was translated by the investigator of the present study in hindi which was checked for its language by the experts on hindi and english. The split half reliability was calculated by dividing the scale into two halves on the basis of odd-even items and it came to be 0.61. This was then boosted for the full length of the scale on Spearman's–Brown Prophecy formula. The reliability of the full scale came to be .75.

Jalota's Group Test of General Mental Ability

To measure Intelligence of the subjects in the sample, the investigator used the hindi version of General Mentai Ability Test constructed and standardized by Jalota (1976). It is for adolescents studying in secondary schools. The test consists of 100 questions spread over five pages and is a group test. Each question is a multiple choice question with five alternatives. The responses are to be given by the subjects on the separate answer sheet. The test is to be completed by the students within 20 minutes. The number of different types of items is given as under:

i)	Synonyms	10 items
ii)	Antonyms	10 items
iii)	Number series	20 items
iv)	Classification	20 items
v)	Appropriate items	10 items
vi)	Reasoning	10 items
vii)	Anologies	20 items

The reliability of this test as reported by the author is 0.94 and the validity ranges from 0.50 to 0.78.

Saxena Adjustment Inventory

For each of the five areas of adjustment, criterion scores were obtained on different sections of Saxena's Adjustment Inventory. It is a paper pencil type test and is intended for use at the school, college and university stages from the age range of 11+ to adulthood. The inventory seeks to discriminate between well adjusted and poorly adjusted persons and provides five separate measures of adjustment namely

Element A	Home Adjustment
Element B	Health Adjustment
Element C	Social Adjustment
Element D	Emotional Adjustment
Element E	Educational Adjustment

Vyaktitiva Parakh Prashnavali contains 90 items. The responses are to be recorded as "yes" or "?" (doubtful) or "No". The items come in a random order and the subject does not know that he is responding for a particular area. The inventory is non- timed, essy to administer and quick to score. It takes about 30 to 40 minutes to answer all the questions. It is suitable for use with both the sexes and can be administered to the individual as well as the group according to the need. A high score on this inventory on each element indicates a superior adjustment while a low score indicates poor adjustment.

Standardization

The inventory has been standardized on a sample of 2529 students of class x to post-graduate level, both males and females. The sample was drawn from the students of arts, science, commerce and teacher training courses representing educational institutions of urban, semi urban and rural areas of eastern, central and western parts of the state of U.P. The sample was divided into four age groups and separate norms have been provided for each group.

Reliability

The reliability co-efficients of the inventory as obtained by various methods range from .87 to .90.

The reliability coefficients of various elements range from .72 to .86 by the test-retest method and from .57 to .84 by the method of rational equivalence.

Validity

The inventory has been correlated with Asthana's Adjustment Inventory and it has given a validity coefficient of .80 on a representative sample of 150 students. This inventory has also been validated against the criterion of teacher's estimate of the personality adjustment of their pupils. The coefficient of correlation between teachers' marks and the scores obtained in the inventory was found to be .63 for boys and .71 for girls.

Extroversion- Introversion Scale

To measure the relative possessiveness of either extraversion or introversion trait by an individual student, Extroversion-Introversion scale developed by Singh and Singh was used. It consists of 56 items in all. Out of these, thirty four are marked with an astrick and twenty-two are without astrick. Each item is to be answered either in "Yes" "No" or "doubtful" but the respondents were asked to avoid doubtful mark. The scale is meant for 16-25 age group. The scale is self-administering and it is mainly for use on groups but it can be administered individually as well. It is useful for both the sexes. There is no time limit for the scale to be completed, though, it may take fifteen minutes for satisfactory completion of this scale.

Reliability

The split half reliability for the scale was reported to be .75 and test-retest.72.

Validity

The scale was validated against external criterion- Jalota and Kapoor's hindi adaptationof Maudsley's Personality Inventory. The validity coefficient was reported to be 0.54.

Socio-Economic Status Scale

In order to gain information about the socio-economic status of the students, the investigator modified the socio-economic status scale developed by Jalota, Pandey, Kapoor and Singh because the original scale appeared to be outdated.

The socio-economic status was assessed by education and income of the family, occupation of parents and living conditions at house which included possession of certain items which have been symbol of varied status. Besides, this scale also gave weightage to the psychological indicators as well as cultural level of the family. The cultural level of the family was judged by expenditure on newspapers, magazines and psychological indicators included the factors as concept of social prestige and belief in caste determining the tendency towards conservatism and progressivism. The scale is meant for urban population only.

Reliability

The coefficient of stability of the modified scale computed by Test-Retest method was found to be 0.95. It showed that the scale was fairly reliable and stable.

Academic Achievement

The aggregate and subject-wise marks obtained by the students in the class IX were treated as an index of their academic-achievement. The marks were converted into the percentages. The investigator got these marks recorded from the cumulative record cards of the students.

Administration of the Tools

It took the investigator two days to administer the tools. On the first day, education interest inventory was administered along with intellectual commitment and socio-economic status scale. On the second day intelligence test, adjustment inventory and extroversion-introversion questionnaires were administered.

Before administering the tests, proper rapport was established with the students. Proper sitting arrangements were made. One student was made to sit on one desk so as to avoid cheating and copying. Before starting each test, directions for completion of the test were read out to the students. Students were informed about the real purpose of the tests and they were asked to give responses freely and honestly with out hiding any thing. A gap of 15 minutes was always given between the completion of a test and start of a new test.

Scoring of the Data

After the collection of data on different tests, it was scored for further analysis and to draw inferences. Scoring of each test was done in accordance with the scoring key given for each test and the scoring keys prepared by the investigator herself.

Scoring Procedure for Educational Interest Inventory

There were seven areas in educational interest inventory. Each area was comprised 25 items which were to be responded on 'L.I.D.' pattern. Two scores were awarded to each response of like (L), one score to each response of indifference (I) and zero score to each response of disliking (D). According to this weightage, area wise total score was counted for each student. The maximum score on each area was 50 and minimum zero. Total score obtained by the student in each area reflected his or her pattern of interest in that area. This pattern of 'L.I.D.' was followed in Strong Vocational Interest Blank (SVIB) and the similar scoring procedure was adapted by Ohio Vocational Interest Survey (OVIS).

Scoring Procedure for Intellectual Commitment Scale

There were nineteen items in all out of which 14 measure commitment and 5 measure non-commitment. Each item was to be scored on five point scale ranging from very true, true, doubtful, false and very false. For the commitment items, five marks were to be given to very true response, four to true response, three to doubtful response, two to false response and one to very false response. The order was reversed in case of non-commitment items.

Scoring Procedure for General Mental Ability Test

There were 100 items in all and one mark was to be given for each correct response. The maximum score can be 100 and minimum zero. The scoring for each item was done in accordance with the directions given in the manual.

Scoring Procedure for Saxena Adjustment Inventory

The answer sheets of the adjustment inventory were scored with the help of five stencil key provided for scoring, there being a separate key for each element of the inventory. For each correctly responded item, one mark was to be given. Neutral responses were ignored.

Scoring Procedure for Extroversion Introversion Scale

Separate scoring procedure was provided both for extroversion and introversion by the author of the test.

Extroversion. 'Yes' mark on questions with astrick mark and 'No' mark on questions marked without astrick were to be counted. One mark for each question mentioned above was to be given. The total marks represented the extroversion category. The maximum score may be 56 and minimum zero.

Introversion. 'No' mark on questions with astrick and 'Yes' mark on questions without astrick were to be counted. One mark for each such question was to be assigned. The total score represented the introversion category of the individual. The maximum possible score might he 56. and minimum zero.

An individual with a very high score, that is, above 75th percentile may be considered an introvert or an extrovert while a person with a very low score, that is, below 25th percentile may be considered as a border line case (insignificant on that trait). The middle group of scores would represent essentially normal individuals, the ambivert type.

Scoring Procedure for Socio-economic Status Scale

There were eleven items in the socio-economic status scale.Scoring of the scale was done in accordance with the scoring key provided and developed by the investigator.

Tabulation and Organization of Data

It consisted of categorization of boys and girls in different categories. After tabulating the scores based on different tests, the investigator made groups by calculating Quartile$_1$, (Q_1) and Quartile$_3$ (Q_3) on different variables *viz.,* intelligence, socio-economic status, intellectual commitment, academic achievement, introversion- extroversion. The values of Q_1 and Q_3 obtained for each variable are shown in table 3.9 alongwith respective number of students falling in each category. The students who fell below Q_1 on different variables were kept in the category of low intelligent, low socio-economic status, low intellectual commitment, low achievers. The students whose scores fell above Q_3 were kept in the category of high intelligent, high socio-economic status, high intellectual commitment, high achievers. Those students whose scores fell in between were kept in the category of average intelligent, middle socio-economic status, average intellectual commitment and average academic achievers. The number of students falling in each of the groups is shown in the following table:

Table 3.5. Number of Students Belonging to Different Groups

Categories	*Boys*	*Girls*	Q_1		Q_3	
			Boys	*Girls*	*Boys*	*Girls*
High Intelligent	63	59			48	45
Average Intelligent	123	130				
Low Intelligent	61	64	24	26		
High SES	61	66			55	59
MSES	125	124				
LSES	61	65	28	37		
High Intellectually Committed	59	62			75	81
Low Intellectually Committed	60	62	65	70		
High Achievers	57	57			49	51
Low Achievers	57	56	29	33		

The investigator also calculated the Q_3 of the extroversion and introversion scores in order to categorize students as extroverted or introverted. Those students who fall above the calculated Q_3 value were categorized as extroverted and introverted. The number of extroverted and introverted boys and girls along with the Q_3 value is given in table:

Table 3.6. Number of Extroverted and Introverted Students

	Number of Students	Q_3
Extroverted	133	28
Introverted	125	27

Categorization was also made on the basis of qualification of father of the students. There were three levels of qualification namely high qualification, average qualification and poor qualification. High qualified were designated as having qualification above B.A., average qualified were designated as having qualification from P.U.C. to B.A. and poor qualified were designated as having qualification matriculation or below matriculation. The number of students belonging to each respective category of father's qualification is shown in the following

Categorization was also made on the basis of qualification of father of the students. There were three levels of qualification namely high qualification, average qualification and poor qualification. High qualified were designated as having qualification above B.A., average qualified were designated as having qualification from P.U.C. to B.A. and poor qualified were designated as having qualification matriculation or below matriculation. The number of students belonging to each respective category of father's qualification is shown in the following:

Table 3.7. Number of Students belonging to Different Categories of Father's Qualification

	High qualified	*Average qualified*	*Poor qualified*
Boys	20	57	170
Girls	31	66	156

The data was further organized on the basis of types of school i.e. govt and private. Here respective number of students falling in each category is gviven in the following table.

Table 3.8. Number of Students belonging to Two Types of Schools

	Govt School	*Private School*
Boys	200	50
Girls	200	50

Zone wise grouping of the students was also done. There were three zones i.e. zone 1, zone 2 and zone 3. Zone 1 represented Jammu, zone 2 represented Udhampur and Kathua and zone 3 represented Poonch and Rajouri. The respective number of boys and girls falling in each zone is shown in table 3.9.

Table 3.9. Number of Students Belonging to Three Zones

	Z_1	Z_2	Z_3
Boys	50	100	100
Girls	50	100	100

Further tabulation was sone in order to categorize subjects into different sub-groups for making further analysis of data. Number of students falling in each respective sub-group is shown in the tables hereafter.

Table 3.10. Number of Students Grouped on the Basis of Types of School and Qualification of Father

	Govt School	*Private School*
High Qualification	29	23
Average Qualification	72	52
Poor Qualification	299	25

Table 3.11. Number of Students Belonging to Different Levels of Sex, Intelligence and Socio-Economic Status

	Boys		*Girls*	
	High Intelli-gent	*Low Intelli-gent*	*High Intelli-gent*	*Low Intelli-gent*
High Socio-Economic Status	29	7	35	7
Middle Socio-Economic Status	27	27	17	35
Low Socio-Economic Status	8	24	7	22

Table 3.12. Number of Students Categorised on the Basis of Extroversion-Introversion, Sex and Intellectual Commitment

	Extroverted		*Introverted*	
	Boys	*Girls*	*Boys*	*Girls*
High Intellectually committed	19	18	9	18
Average Intellectually committed	28	22	22	44
Low Intellectually committed	21	10	13	19

Table 3.13. Number of Students Categorised on the Basis of Extroversion-Introduction, Intellectual Commitment and Academic Achievement

	Extroverted		*Introverted*	
	High Intelle-ctually comm.	*Low Intelle-ctually comm.*	*High Intelle-cutallly comm.*	*Low Intelle-ctually comm.*
High Achievers	10	6	7	6
Low Achievers	8	7	8	10

Since the number of students belonging to different categories was unequal, therefore, the investigator selected the smaller number of subjects from each category for further statistical analysis.

Proposed Statistical Techniques

The investigator made analysis of different types of scores available on various variables for further comparisons and inferences with the help of statistical techniques. The statistical techniques employed in this investigation were mean, standard deviation, quartile deviation, product moment correlation, contingency co-efficient, multiple correlation, analysis of variance, Tukey test, analysis of co-variance, doolittle method of multiple regression analysis, and Kolmogorov-Smirnov test of goodness of fit.

4

Analysis

Introduction

Analysis of data is necessary step in the research process. After the data have been collected, these must be processed and analysed to draw proper inferences. Analysis of data means studying the collected information to determine the inherent facts and meanings. Raw scores don't reveal anything. These are quantitative expression of physical and psychological observations. One can draw proper inferences only after the careful analysis of data. Analysis of data involves breaking down existing complex factors into simpler parts and putting the parts together in new arrangements to discover new factors and relationships for the purpose of interpretations.

According to *Dictionary of Education*, "statistical analysis is the application of statistical process and theory to the compilation, presentation, discussion and interpretation of numerical data" (Good, *et. al.* 1959).

Infact, analysis means the categorising, ordering, manipulating and summarising of data to obtain answers to research questions. The purpose of analysis is to reduce data to intelligible and interpretable form so that the relation of research problem can be studied and tested.

The present chapter deals with analysis of data collected through educational interest inventory (constructed and standardised by the investigator herself), translated version of intellectual commitment scale (Srinivas), group test of general mental ability (Jalota), adjustment inventory (Saxena) personality inventory (Singh and Singh) and modified version of socio-economic status scale (Jalota, *et al.*) The data collected for the present problem have been analysed in the following sections:

The Distribution of Scores

One of the objectives of the present investigation was to study the nature of distribution of scores of seven areas of educational interest and intellectual commitment of boys and girls taken in the sample. Kolmogorov- Smironov method was used to study the goodness of fit of each of the seven areas of educational interest and intellectual commitment scores of the sample, to a normal distribution. This test was preferred to test the normality of the distribution of the scores as in this test, the hypothesis specifies the hypothetical distribution completely, giving the form and the numerical values of all parameters of the distribution. This test is simple to apply and more sensitive than chi- square. The statistic used in this test is based on the maximum difference found between corresponding pairs of cumulative proportions. A simple formula for it is:

$$D= (CPo - CPe)$$

(The Kolmogorov Smirnov maximum deviation statistics)

The computational steps followed for testing the goodness of fit to normal distribution of Intellectual commitment scores are given in table 4.1. Similar steps were followed for testing the goodness of fit of scores in each of the seven areas of educational interest to normal distribution. The obtained D values are given in table 4.2.

The Educational Interest Patterns

In this section, the educational interest patterns of different groups of students were studied. Grouping was done on the basis of sex, zones, govt and private school, qualification of parents, extra

Table 4.1. Testing goodness of fit of intellectual commitment scores

Scores	*f*	*Cum f*	CP_0	CP_e	CP_0-CP_e
90–94	4	500	1.000	.996	.004
85–89	26	496	0.992	.981	.011
80–84	69	470	0.940	.929	.011
75–79	108	401	0.802	.805	–.003
70–74	113	293	0.586	.598	–.012
65–69	106	180	0.360	.363	–.003
60–64	48	74	0.148	.168	–.020
55–59	14	26	0.052	.058	–.006
50–54	6	12	0.024	.014	.014
45–49	6	6	0.012	.002	.010

D= .02

1.36 / √500 at the level of P = .05 i.e. 1.36/22.36 = .608.

Table 4.2. D values for seven areas of educational interest

Areas	*Ag.*	*F.A.*	*Com.*	*Hum.*	*Home Sci.*	*Sci.*	*Tech*
D =	.03	.01	.04	.02	.05	.05	.02

Table 4.3. Mean Values of Educational Interest Scores of Boys and Girls

Areas of Educa-tional Interest	*Boys*		*Girls*	
	Mean	*Rank*	*Mean*	*Rank*
Agriculure	31.55	4	24.68	5
Fine Arts	25.91	6	25.2	4
Commerce	29.53	5	22.47	7
Humanities	32.77	2	29.04	3
Home Science	23.93	7	37.82	1
Science	36.77	1	35.84	2
Technology	32.00	3	23.00	6

version- introversion, intellectual commitment, academic achievement, intelligence and socio- economic status. For studying the patterns of educational interest, mean, which is a measure of descriptive statistics was applied. The rank positions were assigned to each interest area on the basis of mean values for better understanding. The mean values of seven areas of educational interest with respect to different groups along with rank positions are given in tables 4.3 to 4.11.

Table 4.4. Mean Values of Educational Interest Scores of Students Belonging to Three Zones

Areas of Educational Interest	*Jammu (Z_1)*		*Udhampur Kathua Z_2*		*Poonch Rajouri Z_3*	
	Mean	*Rank*	*Mean*	*Rank*	*Mean*	*Rank*
Agriculture	24.7	7	30.73	3	28.93	4
Fine Arts	26.53	4	26.23	7	24.90	7
Commerce	25.76	5	26.70	6	25.53	6
Humanities	31.03	2	30.60	4	31.10	3
Home Science	25.30	6	34.0	2	33.36	2
Science	35.16	1	34.93	1	34.81	1
Technology	28.23	3	27.50	5	27.83	5

Table 4.5. Mean Values of Educational Interest Scores of Students Studying in Government and Private Schools

Areas of Educational Interest	*Govt. School*		*Private School*	
	Mean	*Rank*	*Mean*	*Rank*
Agriculure	26.29	5	24.08	7
Fine Arts	26.82	4	26.38	5
Commerce	25.89	6	27.05	4
Humanities	29.66	3	29.64	2
Home Science	35.16	2	24.33	6
Science	37.12	1	32.82	1
Technology	24.44	7	29.09	3

Table 4.6. Mean Values of Educational Interest Scores of Students Belonging to Three Levels of Father's Qualification

Areas of Educational Interest	*High Qualification*		*Average Qualification*		*Poor Qualification*	
	Mean	*Rank*	*Mean*	*Rank*	*Mean*	*Rank*
Agriculture	25.76	7	25.44	5	25.36	7
Fine Arts	28.40	5	25.78	4	25.64	6
Commerce	28.32	6	24.36	6	26.74	4
Humanities	32.72	2	26.98	3	28.82	3
Home Science	32.60	3	27.06	2	29.58	2
Science	35.88	1	35.00	1	34.04	1
Technology	28.58	4	25.24	5	26.48	5

Table 4.7. Mean Values of Educational Interest Scores of Extroverted and Introverted Students

Areas of Educational Interest	*Extroverted*		*Introverted*	
	Mean	*Rank*	*Mean*	*Rank*
Agriculure	27.12	7	27.12	6
Fine Arts	27.20	6	26.29	7
Commerce	27.87	5	27.83	4
Humanities	34.83	2	33.19	3
Home Science	34.45	3	34.16	2
Science	39.00	1	36.79	1
Technology	31.00	4	27.00	5

Table 4.8. Mean Values of Educational Interest Scores of Students Belonging to Levels of Intellectual Commitment

Areas of Educational Interest	*High Intellectually Committed*		*Low Intellectually Committed*	
	Mean	*Rank*	*Mean*	*Rank*
Agriculure	26.83	7	27.41	5
Fine Arts	26.72	6	26.66	7
Commerce	28.66	5	·27.04	6
Humanities	35.04	3	33.08	2
Home Science	35.91	2	32.70	3
Science	40.92	1	34.86	1
Technology	29.79	4	28.83	4

Table 4.9. Mean Values of Educational Interest Scores of High Achievers and Low Achievers

Areas of Educational Interest	*High Achievers*		*Low Achievers*	
	Mean	*Rank*	*Mean*	*Rank*
Agriculure	25.00	6	29.25	6
Fine Arts	24.16	7	29.33	5
Commerce	26.21	5	29.5	4
Humanities	33.91	2	34.20	3
Home Science	29.04	4	39.58	1
Science	38.86	1	36.92	2
Technology	30.25	3	28.37	7

Table 4.10 Mean Values of Educational Interest Scores of Students Belonging to the Levels of Intelligence

Areas of Educational Interest	*High Intelligent*		*Low Intelligent*	
	Mean	*Rank*	*Mean*	*Rank*
Agriculure	28.09	4	29.33	4
Fine Arts	25.56	7	26.61	5
Commerce	25.83	6	26.5	6
Humanities	31.76	2	30.76	3
Home Science	30.38	3	32.95	2
Science	38.90	1	37.38	1
Technology	26.76	5	25.36	7

The Significance of Means Difference

In this section, the objective to be realised was to study the significance of means difference in the intellectual commitment and educational interest scores of students in relation to different variables under study. The interactional effect of different variables on means difference in intellectual commitment and educational interest scores was also studied.

Table 4.11. Mean Values of Educational Interest Scores of Students Belonging to Three Levels of Socio-Economic Status

Areas of Educational Interest	*High Socio-Eco. Status*		*Middle Socio-Eco. Status*		*Low Socio-Eco. Status*	
	Mean	*Rank*	*Mean*	*Rank*	*Mean*	*Rank*
Agriculture	24.36	7	30.92	4	30.71	4
Fine Arts	25.21	6	25.86	7	27.21	5
Commerce	25.89	5	27.57	5	25.03	7
Humanities	30.21	2	31.86	3	31.71	3
Home Science	26.96	3	32.42	2	35.43	2
Science	37.35	1	41.03	1	36.03	1
Technology	26.00	4	26.68	6	25.5	6

In order to ascertain whether the obtained means of different criterions (in relation to independent variables) differed significantly from one another, analysis of variance technique developed by R.A. Fisher (1934) was applied.' 't' test tells us about the significance of difference between the mean values of two small random samples. In the present investigation, there were 6,8 and 12 sets of measurements for many experimental designs. Application of 't' test would have involved lots of time and energy. In this situation, it was considered desirable to have some overall test of several samples simultaneously to know whether any of the differences were significant. Analysis of variance technique compares mean values of more than two sets of measurement by a single test called F-Test. It is based on individual differences and presents a global picture of the effect of different treatments on criterion scores.

The assumptions of normality and homogeneity underlying analysis of variance were not tested for the various factorial designs of the present study. For the assumption of normality, Eden and Yates, as quoted by Johnson (1961) showed that even with a population departing considerably from normality, the effectiveness of z- distribution still held. Besides this finding, the conclusion of

Norton's study is also important. Norton as quoted by Guilford (1965) found that F is rather insensitive to variations in shape of population distribution. In the light of these findings it was not considered necessary to test the data of various factorial designs for normality.

F- test is also quite insensitive to the heterogeneity of variance, provided that there are equal number of observations for each treatment Box (1953). Keeping in view the assertion of Box (1953) for testing homogeneity of variance, it was, therefore, not essential to test this assumption.

The requirement of randomness for various factorial designs was amply fulfilled in this study as the sample was random and subjects were further randomly assigned to varied experimental groups from the sample.

The F- ratios obtained on various experimental designs of Anova were checked for their significance. On finding F- ratios for the main effects or interactions to be significant, the test developed by Tukey (1949) was applied to see the levels of the factors which caused significance.

't' values calculated following significant F- ratios for the main and interactional effects of different factors are presented in tabular form in their respective sections. The level of significance for testing the significance of means difference was only .05 as has been already said in first chapter. The verification of hypotheses was done only at this level of significance even when those were significant at. 01 level.

This section has further been classified into eight sub- sections. The analysis of each sub- section is presented in the following pages:

Significance of Means Difference in the Educational Interest Scores in Relation to Sex and Zones

One of the objectives of the study was to study the significance of means difference in the educational interest scores of the students in relation to sex and zones. Seven areas of educational interest were taken up separately. Since effect of two independent variables was to be seen on one criterion, two- way analysis of variance technique was applied. All the sets were equated by randomly selecting 15 cases from each set of design. Since there were two types of sex and three types of zones, 2×3 factorial design was prepared as given below:

Paradigm of experiment

Sex	Boys	Girls	
A	A_1	A_2	
Zones	zone1	$zone_2$	$zone_3$
B	B_1	B_2	B_3

The outcome of analysis of variance for each area of educational interest has been presented in various tables hereafter:

Table 4.12. Summary of 2x3 Factorial Design for Agriculture Area of Educational Interest

Sources of Variation	*Sum of Squares*	*df*	*Mean Variance*	*F-ratio*	*Significance*
Main Effects					
A	106.90	1	106.90	18.36	Significant
B	575.62	2	287.81	5.06	Significant
First order Interaction					
AxB	548.60	2	274.30	4.83	Significant
Within	470.53	84	56.79		
		89			

Table 4.13. Mean Values of Interest in Agriculture

	A_1	A_2	
B_1	25.86	25.53	24.7
B_2	33	28.46	30.73
B_3	35.80	20.06	28.93
	31.55	24.68	

Table 4.13 (a) Testing Significance of the Levels of Factor B

Levels of factor B	*N*	*Obtained 't' ratios*	*Required sig. 't' ratio at 0.5 level*	*Significance*
B_1 vs. B_2	30	3.11	2.04	Significant

The mean difference required for significance between any two pairs of the levels of factor B should be 3.96 or more. Mean difference between all other pairs of different levels were less than this stated value. Hence there was no need to calculate 't' values for rest of the pairs.

Table 4.13 (b) Testing Significance of the Levels of A×B Interaction

Levels of Interaction A×B	*N*	*Obtained 't' ratio*	*Required signif.cant ratio at .05 level*	*Significance*
A_1B_3 vs A_2B_3	15	5.72	2.14	Significant
A_1B_3 vs A_2B_1		3.73		Significant
A_1B_3 vs. A_1B_1		3.61		Significant
A_1B_3 vs. A_2B_2		2.66		Significant
A_1B_2 vs. A_2B_3		4.70		Significant
A_1B_2 vs. A_2B_1		2.71		Significant
A_1B_2 vs. A_1B_1		2.59		Significant
A_2B_2 vs. A_2B_3		3.05		Significant

Table 4.14. Summary of 2×3 Factorial Design for Fine Arts Area of Educational Interest

Sources of Variation	*Sum of Squares*	*df*	*Mean Variance*	*F-ratio*	*Significance*
Main effects					
A	11.37	1	11.37	0.18	Insignificant
B	44.68	2	22.34	0.35	Insignificant
First order Interaction					
A×B	54.82	2	27.41	0.32	Insignificant
Within	5305.33	84	63.15		
		89			

Table 4.15. Mean Values of Interest in Fine Arts

	A_1	A_2	
B_1	26.00	27.06	26.53
B_2	26.60	25.86	26.23
B_3	25.13	24.67	24.9
	25.91	25.86	

Table 4.16. Summary of 2×3 Factorial Design for Commerce Area of Educational Interest

Sources of Variation	*Sum of Squares*	*df*	*Mean Variance*	*F-ratio*	*Significance*
Main Effects					
A	1123.60	1	1123.60	13.19	Significant
B	22.87	2	11.45	0.13	Insignificant
First order Interaction					
A×B	160.06	2	80.03	0.93	Insignificant
Within	7153.46	84	85.16		
		89			

The mean difference required for significance between any two pairs of the lavels of A×B interaction should be 5.98 or more. Mean difference between all others pairs of different levels were less than this stated value. Hence there was no need to calculate 't' values for rest of the pairs.

Table 4.17. Mean Values of Interest in Commerce

	A_1	A_2	
B_1	28.6	22.93	25.76
B_2	29.06	24.33	26.70
B_3	30.93	20.13	25.53
	29.53	22.46	

Table 4.18. Summary of 2x3 Factorial Design for Humanities Area of Educational Interest

Sources of Variation	*Sum of Squares*	*df*	*Mean Variance*	*F-ratio*	*Significance*
Main Effects					
A	313.60	1	313.60	3.51	Insignificant
B	4.42	2	2.21	0.02	Insignificant
First order Interaction					
A×B	444.60	2	222.3	2.49	Insignificant
Within	7484.66	84	89.10		
		89			

Table 4.19. Mean Values of Interest in Humanities

	A_1	A_2	
B_1	31.8	30.26	31.03
B_2	30.46	30.73	30.06
B_3	36.06	26.13	31.10
	32.77	29.04	

Table 4.20. Summary of 2×3 Factorial Design for Home Science Area of Educational Interest

Sources of Variation	*Sum of Squares*	*df*	*Mean Variance*	*F-ratio*	*Significance*
Main Effects					
A	4326.40.	1	4326.40	51.93	Significant
B	1411.62	2	705.81	8.48	Significant
First order Interaction					
A×B	432.46	2	216.23	2.59	Insignificant
Within	6990.40	84	83.21		
		89			

Table 4.21. Mean Values of Interest in Home Science

	A_1	A_2	
B_1	18.46	32.13	25.3
B_2	24.33	43.67	34
B_3	29.06	37.67	33.37
	23.95	37.82	-

Table 4.21(a).Testing Significance of the Levels of Factor B

Levels of factor B	*N*	*Obtained 't' ratios*	*Required sig. 't' ratio at 0.5 level*	*Significance*
B_1 vs. B_2	30	3.69	2.04	Significant
B_1vs. B_3		3.57		Significant

The mean difference required for significance between any two pairs of the levels of factor B should be 4.81 or more. 't' test was not applied on the pair B_2 VS. B_3 as the gap between the means of this pair was less than 4.81.

Table 4.22. Summary of 2×3 Factorial Design for Science Area of Educational Interest

Sources of Variation	*Sum of Squares*	*df*	*Mean Variance*	*F-ratio*	*Significance*
Main Effects					
A	19.60	1	19.60	0.17	Insignificant
B	567.08	2	283.54	2.54	Insignificant
First order Interaction					
A×B	127.40	2	63.7	0.57	Insignificant
Within	9407.20	84	111.20		
		89			

Table 4.23. Mean Values of Interest in Science

	A_1	A_2	
B_1	34.8	33.53	34.16
B_2	33.86	36	34.93
B_3	41.67	38	39.83
	36.77	35.84	

Table 4.24. Summary of 2×3 Factorial Design for Technology Area of Educational Interest

Sources of Variation	*Sum of Squares*	*df*	*Mean Variance*	*F-ratio*	*Significance*
Main Effects					
A	1932.10	1	1932.10	19.66	Significant
B	8.08	2	4.04	0.04	Insignificant
First order Interaction					
A×B	416.27	2	208.13	2.11	Insignificant
Within	8254.63	84	98.27		
		89			

Table 4.25. Mean Values of Interest in Technology

	A_1	A_2	
B_1	30.27	26.2	28.23
B_2	32.06	22.93	27.5
B_3	35.13	20.53	27.83
	32.49	23.22	

Significance of means difference in the educational interest scores in relation to types of school and father's qualification

In this sub-section, significance of means difference in the educational interest scores of students studying in two types of school and belonging to three levels of father's qualification was analysed. Seven areas of Educational interest were taken up separately. All the sets were equated by randomly selecting 25 students from each set of the design. Since there were two types of school and three levels of father's qualification, 2×3 factorial design was set up as presented below:

Paradigm of Experiment

Types of School	*Govt. School*		*Private School*
A		A_1	A_2
Qualification	High Qualification	Average Qualification	Low Qualification
B	B_1	B_2	B_3

The outcome of hypothetical experiment for each area of educational interest has been given through tables 4.26 to 4.39 which have been presented hereafter.

Table 4.26. Summary of 2×3 Factorial Design for Agriculture Area of Educational Interest

Sources of Variation	*Sum of Squares*	*df*	*Mean Variance*	*F-ratio*	*Significance*
Main Effects					
A	89.71	1	89.71	8.62	Insignificant
B	4.48	2	2.24	0.02	Insignificant
First order Interaction					
A×B	425.81	2	212.90	2.59	Insignificant
Within	11811.44	144	82.02		
		149			

Table 4.27. Mean Values of Interest in Agriculture

	A_1	A_2	
B_1	28.24	23.28	25.76
B_2	26.8	24.08	25.44
B_3	23.84	26.88	25.36
	26.29	24.74	

Table 4.28. Summary of 2×3 Factorial Design for Fine Arts Area of Educational Interest

Sources of Variation	*Sum of Squares*	*df*	*Mean Variance*	*F-ratio*	*Significance*
Main Effects					
A	7.26	1	7.26	0.12	Insignificant
B	241.69	2	120.83	1.92	Insignificant
First order Interaction					
A×B	384.75	2	192.38	3.06	Significant
Within	9060.07	144	62.91		
		149			

Table 4.29. Mean Values of Interest in Fine Arts

	A_1	A_2	
B_1	30.88	25.92	28.4
B_2	25	26.56	25.78
B_3	24.6	26.68	25.64
	26.82	26.39	

Table 4.29 (a) Testing Significance of the Levels of A×B Interaction

Levels of Interaction A×B	*N*	*Obtained 't' ratios*	*Required significant 't' ratio at 0.5 level*	*Significance*
A_1B_1 vs A_1B_3	25	2.80	2.06	Significant
A_1B_1 vs. A_1B_2		2.35		Significant
A_1B_1 vs. A_2B_1		2.21		Significant

The means difference required for significance between any two pairs of the levels of A×B interactions should be 4.61 or more. The means difference between all other pairs of different levels were less than this stated value. Hence 't' values were not calculated for rest of the pairs.

Table 4.30. Summary of 2×3 Factorial Design for Commerce Area of Educational Interest

Sources of Variation	*Sum of Squares*	*df*	*Mean Variance*	*F-ratio*	*Significance*
Main Effects					
A	50.50	1	50.50	0.64	Insignificant
B	397.37	2	198.69	2.51	Insignificant
First order Interaction					
A×B	253.66	2	128.78	1.60	Insignificant
Within	1396	144	79.13		
		149			

Table 4.31. Mean Values of Interest in Commerce

	A_1	A_2	
B_1	29.28	27.36	28.32
B_2	23.88	24.84	24.36
B_3	24.52	28.95	26.74
	25.89	27.05	

Table 4.32. Summary of 2x3 Factorial Design for Humanities Area of Educational Interest

Sources of Variation	*Sum of Squares*	*df*	*Mean Variance*	*F-ratio*	*Signific-ance*
Main Effects					
A	3.84	1	3.84	0.05	Insignificant
B	859.05	2	429.52	5.71	Significant
First order Interaction					
A×B	601.32	2	300.65	4.00	Significant
Within	10815.25	144	75.11		
		149			

Table 4.33. Mean Values of Interest in Humanities

	A_1	A_2	
B_1	35.12	30.32	32.72
B_2	27.52	26.44	26.98
B_3	26.32	31.28	28.82
	29.66	29.34	

Table 4.33 (a) Testing Significance of the Levels of Factor B

Levels of Factor B	*N*	*Obtained 't' ratios*	*Required significant 't' ratio at 0.5 level*	*Significance*
B_1vs.B_2	50	3.30	2.01	Significant
B_1vs.B_3		2.24		Significant

The mean difference required for significance between any two pairs of the levels of factor B should be 3.50 or more. 't' test was not applied on the pair B_2 vs. B_3 as the difference between the means of this pair was less than 3.50.

Table 4.33 (b) Testing Significance of the Levels of A×B Interactions

Levels of Interaction A×B	*N*	*Obtained 't' ratios*	*Required significant 't' ratio at 0.5 level*	*Significance*
A_1B_1 vs. A_1B_3	25	3.57	2.06	Significant
A_1B_1 vs. A_2B_2		3.54		Significant
A_1B_1 vs. A_1B_2		3.10		Significant

The mean difference required for significance between any two pairs of the levels of A×B interaction should be 5.05 or more. The mean difference between all other pairs of different levels were less than this stated values. Hence 't' values were not calculated for rest of the pairs.

Table 4.34. Summary of 2×3 Factorial Design for Home Science Area of Educational Interest

Sources of Variation	*Sum of Squares*	*df*	*Mean Variance*	*F-ratio*	*Significance*
Main Effects					
A	4395.63	1	4395.63	31.60	Significant
B	769.37	2	384.68	2.76	Inignificant
First order Interaction					
A×B	181.45	2	90.72	0.65	Insignificant
Within	20031.92	144	139.11		
		149			

Table 4.35. Mean Values of Interest in Home Science

	A_1	A_2	
B_1	38.72	26.48	32.6
B_2	33.32	20.8	27.05
B_3	33.34	25.72	29.58
	35.16	24.33	

Table 4.36. Summary of 2×3 Factorial Design for Science Area of Educational Interest

Sources of Variation	*Sum of Squares*	*df*	*Mean Variance*	*F-ratio*	*Significance*
Main Effects					
A	691.23	1	691.23	6.63	Significant
B	84.69	2	42.34	0.19	Inignificant
First order Interaction					
A×B	427.57	2	213.78	2.04	Insignificant
	15022.40	144	104.32		
		149			

Table 4.37. Mean Values of Interest in Science

	A_1	A_2	
B_1	35.64	36.12	35.88
B_2	38.4	31.6	35
B_3	37.52	30.76	34.04
	37.12	32.82	

Table 4.38. Summary of 2×3 Factorial Design for Technology Area of Educational Interest

Sources of Variation	*Sum of Squares*	*df*	*Mean Variance*	*F-ratio*	*Significance*
Main Effects					
A	812.00	1	812.0	8.42	Significant
B	285.05	2	142.52	1.47	Inignificant
First order Interaction					
A×B	288.65	2	144.32	1.50	Insignificant
Within	13879.11	144	96.38		
		149			

Table 4.39. Mean Values of Interest in Technology.

	A_1	A_2	
B_1	28.16	29	28.58
B_2	22.36	28.12	25.24
B_3	22.8	30.16	26.48
24.44	29.03		

Significance of Means Difference in the Educational Interest Scores in Relation to Extraversion- Introversion Intellectual commitment and Academic Achievement

In this sub-section, the significance of means difference in the educational interest scores in relation to extraversion- introversion, intellectual commitment and academic achievement was studied. As the effect of three independent variables was to be seen on one criterion, three way analysis of variance technique was applied. All the sets were equated by randomly selecting 6 cases from each sets of the design. Since there were two levels of each variable, 2×2×2 factorial design was prepared as given follow:

Paradigm of Experiment

Extraversion Introversion *A*	*Extraversion* A_1	*Interoversion* A_2
Intellectual commitment B	High Intellectually committed B_1	Low Intellectually committed B_2
Academic Achievement C	High Achievers C_1	Low achievers C_2

The outcome of this hypothetical experiment for seven areas of educational interest have been given in the following tables.

Table 4.40. Summary of 2×2×2 Factorial Design for Agriculture Area of Educational Interest

Sources of Variation	*Sum of Squares*	*df*	*Mean Variance*	*F-ratio*	*Signific-ance*
Main Effects					
A	0	1	0	0	Insignificant
B	4.08	1	216.75	2.09	Inignificant
First order Interaction					
A×B	56.33	1	56.33	0.54	Insignificant
A× C	385.33	1	385.33	3.72	Insignificant
B × C	290.08	1	290.08	2.79	Insignificant
Second Order Interaction					
A×B×C	133.33	1	133.33	1.28	Insignificant
Within	4145.33	40	103.63		
		49			

Table 4.41. Mean Values of Interest in Agriculture

	A_1		A_2		
	B_1	B_2	B_1	B_2	
C_1	16.67	27.67	27.03	27.03	25.00
C_2	34.83	29.33	28.	24.83	29.25
	25.75	28.50	27.91	26.33	

A_1=27.12 B_1 = 26.83

A_2=27.12 B_2 = 27.41

Table 4.42. Summary of 2x2x2 Factorial Design for Fine Arts Area of Educational Interest

Sources of Variation	*Sum of Squares*	*df*	*Mean Variance*	*F-ratio*	*Significance*
Main Effects					
A	10.08	1	1 0.08	0.14	Insignificant
B	0.33	1	0.33	0.00	Inignificant
C	320.33	1	320.33	4.60	Significant
First order Interaction					
A×B	60.75	1	60.75	0.87	Insignificant
A× C	60.75	1	60.75	0.87	Insignificant
B × C	208.33	1	208.33	2.79	Insignificant
Second Order Interaction					
A×B×C	154.08	1	154.08	2.21	Insignificant
Within	2784.33	40	69.60		
		47			

Table 4.43. Mean Values of Interest in Fine Arts

	A_1		A_2		
	B_1	B_2	B_1	B_2	
C_1	20.8	30.66	23.5	21.67	24.16
C_2	31.5	25.83	31.5	28.5	29.33
	26.14	28.25	27.5	25.08	

A_1=27.20 B_1 = 26.82

A_2=26.29 B_2 = 26.66

Table 4.44. Summary of 2×2×2 Factorial Design for Commerce Area of Educational Interest

Sources of Variation	*Sum of Squares*	*df*	*Mean Variance*	*F-ratio*	*Significance*
Main Effects					
A	0.02	1	0.02	0.00	Insignificant
B	31.68	1	31.68	0.33	Inignificant
C	130.02	1	130.02	1.38	Insignifcant
First order Interaction					
A×B	17.52	1	17.52	0.18	Insignificant
A× C	111.02	1	111.02	1.18	Insignificant
B × C	346.69	1	346.69	3.70	Insignificant
Second Order Interaction					
A×B×C	28.52	1	28.52	0.30	Insignificant
Within	3745.5	40	93.66		
		47			

Table 4.45. Mean Values of Interest in Commerce

	A_1		A_2		
	B_1	B_2	B_1	B_2	
C_1	24.5	31	24.15	25.17	26.20
C_2	31.67	24.33	34.33	27.67	29.5
	28.08	27.66	29.25	26.42	

A_1=27.87 B_1 = 28.67

A_2=27.83 B_2 = 27.04

Table 4.46. Summary of 2×2×2 Factorial Design for Humanities Area of Educational Interest

Sources of Variation	*Sum of Squares*	*df*	*Mean Variance*	*F-ratio*	*Signific-ance*
Main Effects					
A	28.52	1	28.52	0.26	Insignificant
B	46.02	1	46.02	0.48	Inignificant
C	1.02	1	1.02	0.00	Insignificant
First order Interaction					
A×B	42.19	1	42.19	0.39	Insignifi-cant
A× C	315.18	1	315.18	2.98	Insignificant
B × C	188.02	1	188.02	1.78	Insignificant
Second Order Interaction					
A×B×C	6.02	1	6.02	0.05	Insignificant
Within	4225.83	40	105.64		
		47			

Table 4.47. Mean Values of Interest in Humanities

	A_1		A_2		
	B_1	B_2	B_1	B_2	
C_1	36.83	31.67	29	32.17	33.91
C_2	36.66	28.17	37.66	34.33	34.20
	36.75	32.92	33.33	33.25	
	A_1=34.83		B_1 = 35.04		
	A_2=33.29		B_2 = 33.08		

Table 4.48. Summary of 2x2x2 Factorial Design for Home Science Area of Educational Interest

Sources of Variation	*Sum of Squares*	*df*	*Mean Variance*	*F-ratio*	*Significance*
Main Effects					
A	1.02	1	1.02	0.00	Insignificant
B	123.52	1	123.52	0.79	Inignificant
C	1333.52	1	1333.52	0.54	Insignificant
First order Interaction					
A×B	38.52	1	38.52	0.25	Insignificant
A× C	7.52	1	7.52	0.05	Insignificant
B × C	31.69	1	31.69	0.20	Insignificant
Second Order Interaction					
A×B×C	63.02	1	63.02	0.40	Insignificant
Within	6239.5	40	155.98		
		47			

Table 4.49. Mean Values of Interest in Home-Science

	A_1		A_2		
	B_1	B_2	B_1	B_2	
C_1	28.33	30.83	31.33	25.67	29.04
C_2	42	36.67	42	37.66	39.58
	35.16	33.75	36.66	31.67	
	A_1=34.45		B_1 = 35.91		
	A_2=34.16		B_2 = 32.71		

Table 4.50. Summary of 2×2×2 Factorial Design for Science Area of Educational Interest

Sources of Variation	*Sum of Squares*	*df*	*Mean Variance*	*F-ratio*	*Significance*
Main Effects					
A	58.82	1	50.82	0.56	Insignificant
B	438.02	1	438.02	4.20	Significant
C	46.02	1	46.02	0.44	Insignifcant
First order Interaction					
A×B	46.02	1	46.02	0.44	Insignificant
A× C	136.69	1	136.69	1.31	Insignificant
B × C	9.19	1	9.19	0.08	Insignificant
Second Order Interaction					
A×B×C	7.52	1	7.52	0.07	Insignificant
Within	4170.05	40	104.26		
		47			

Table 4.51. Mean Values of Interest in Science

	A_1		A_2		
	B_1	B_2	B_1	B_2	
C_1	46.5	36.83	38.17	34	38.87
C_2	39.5	33.16	38	35	36.54
43	35	38.08	34.75		

$A_1 = 39$ $B_1 = 40.54$

$A_2 = 36.41$ $B_2 = 34.87$

Table 4.52. Summary of 2×2×2 Factorial Design in Technology Area of Educational Interest

Sources of Variation	*Sum of Squares*	*df*	*Mean Variance*	*F-ratio*	*Significance*
Main Effects					
A	247.52	1	247.52	1.9	Insignificant
B	11.02	1	11.02	0.08	Insignificant
C	42.19	1	42.19	0.33	Insignificant
First order Interaction					
A×B	6.02	1	6.02	0.44	Insignificant
A× C	54.19	1	54.19	0.52	Insignificant
B × C	426.02	1	426.02	0.98	Insignificant
Second Order Interaction					
A×B×C	15.19	1	15.19	0.11	Insignificant
Within	5126.17	40	128.15		
		47			

Table 4.53. Mean Values of Interest in Technology

	A_1		A_2		
	B_1	B_2	B_1	B_2	
C_1	46.5	36.83	38.17	34	38.87
C_1	32	35.16	24.5	30.33	30.49
C_2	32.83 26.33	30.83	23.5	28.37	
	32.41 30.74	27.66	26.91		

$A_1 = 31.57$ $B_1 = 30.03$

$A_2 = 27.28$ $B_2 = 28.82$

Significance of Means Difference in Educational Interest Scores in Relation to Sex, Intelligence and Socio- Economic Status

In this sub- section, the objective was to study the significance of means difference in the educational interest scores in relation to sex, intelligence and socio- economic status. As there were three independent variables to influence the criterion, three way analysis of variance technique was applied. All the sets were equated by randomly selecting seven cases from each set of the design. 2×2×3 factorial design was prepared as given below:

Paradigm of Experiment

Sex	*Boys*		*Girls*
A	A_1		A_2
Intelligence	High Intelligent		Low Intelligent
B	B_1		B_2
Socio-Economic Status	High SES	Middle SES	Low SES
C	C_1	C_2	C_3

The out come of this hypothetical experiment for each of the seven areas of educational interest has been presented in tables 4.54 to 4.67.

Table 4.54. Summary of 2x2x3 Factorial Design for Agriculture Area of Educational Interest

Sources of Variation	*Sum of Squares*	*df*	*Mean Variance*	*F-ratio*	*Significance*
Main Effects					
A	9.33	1	9.33	0.11	Insignificant
B	27.43	1	27.43	0.34	Insignificant
C	780.66	2	390.33	4.80	Significant
First order Interaction					
A×B	42.86	1	42.86	0.54	Insignificant
A× C	1550.09	2	775.04	9.69	Significant
B × C	434.00	2	217.00	2.71	Insignificant
Second Order Interaction					
A×B×C	80.86	2	40.43	0.50	Insignificant
Within	5755.43	72	79.94		
		83			

Table 4.55. Mean Values of Interest in Agriculture

	A_1		A_2		
	B_1	B_2	B_1	B_2	
C_1	15.71	21.57	30.43	29.57	24.31
C_2	29.71	37.00	26.68	29.86	30.71
C_3	37.71	31.43	28.71	25.00	30.71
	27.71	30.00	28.47	28.14	

A_1= 28.86 B_1 = 28.09
A_2= 28.31 B_2 = 29.07

Table 4.55 (a). Testing Significance of the Levels of Factor C

Levels of Factor C	*N*	*Obtained 't' ratios*	*Required significant 't' ratio at 0.5 level*	*Significance*
C_1vs. C_2	28	2.68	2.05	Significant
C_1vs. C_3		2.68		Significant

The mean difference required for significance between any two pairs of the levels of factor C should be 4.90 or more. 't' test was not applied on the pair C_2 vs C_3 as there was no difference in the means of this pairs

Table 4.55 (b) Testing Significance of the Levels of A×C Interaction

Levels of Factor A×C	*N*	*Obtained 't' ratios*	*Required significant 't' ratio at 0.5 level*	*Significance*
A_1C_3vs. A_1C_1	14	3.33	2.45	Significant
A_1C_1vs.A_1 C_1		3.07		Significant

The mean difference required for significance between any two pairs of the levels of A× C should be 11.71 or more. 't' values were not calculated for the remaining pairs as the mean difference between the remaining pairs was less than the stated value of 11.71.

The mean difference required for significance between any two pairs of the levels of A × C interaction should be 13.08 more. 't' values were not calculated for the remaining pairs as the mean difference between rest of the pairs were less than 13.08.

Table 4.56. Summary of 2x2x3 Factorial Design for Fine Arts Area of Educational Interest

Sources of Variation	*Sum of Squares*	*df*	*Mean Variance*	*F-ratio*	*Significance*
Main Effects					
A	149.33	1	149.33	1.63	Insignificant
B	23.04	1	23.04	0.25	Insignificant
C	58.38	2	29.19	0.32	Insignificant
First order Interaction					
A×B	4.76	1	4.76	0.05	Insignificant
A× C	314.95	2	157.47	1.73	Insignificant
B × C	80.67	2	40.34	0.44	Insignificant
Second Order Interaction					
A×B×C	84.09	2	42.04	0.46	Insignificant
Within	6568	72	91.11		
		83			

Table 4.57. Mean Values of Interest in Fine Arts

	A_1		A_2		
	B_1	B_2	B_1	B_2	
C_1	19.28	23	29.57	29	25.21
C_2	24.71	27	23.86	27.86	25.86
C_3	29.42	25.14	26.57	27.71	27.21
	24.47	25.05	26.67	28.19	

A_1= 24.76 B_1 = 25.57

A_2= 27.43 B_2 = 26.62

Table 4.58. Summary of 2×2×3 Factorial Design for Commerce Area of Educational Interest

Sources of Variation	*Sum of Squares*	*df*	*Mean Variance*	*F-ratio*	*Significance*
Main Effects					
A	525.0	1	525.0	5.90	Significant
B	9.33	1	9.33	0.10	Insignificant
C	93.17	2	46.58	0.52	Insignificant
First order Interaction					
A×B	61.71	1	61.71	0.69	Insignificant
A× C	546.73	2	273.46	3.08	Insignificant
B × C	258.02	2	129.01	1.45	Insignificant
Second Order Interaction					
A×B×C	103.79	2	51.89	0.58	Insignificant
Within	6397.71	72	88.55		
		83			

Table 4.59. Mean Values of Interest in Fine Arts

	A_1		A_2		
	B_1	B_2	B_1	B_2	
C_1	22.14	27.71	27.28	26.43	25.89
C_2	29.71	32.14	21.57	26.85	27.57
C_3	30.57	29.71	23.71	16.14	25.03
	27.47	29.85	24.18	23.14	

A_1= 28.66 B_1 = 25.82

A_2= 23.67 B_2 = 26.5

Table 4.60. Summary of 2x2x3 Factorial Design for Humanities Area of Educational Interest

Sources of Variation	*Sum of Squares*	*df*	*Mean Variance*	*F-ratio*	*Significance*
Main Effects					
A	233.33	1	233.33	2.17	Insignificant
B	21.0	1	21.0	0.19	Insignificant
C	46.39	2	23.19	0.21	Insignifcant
First order Interaction					
AxB	42.85	1	21.43	0.20	Insignificant
Ax C	408.67	2	204.34	1.91	Insignificant
B x C	378.29	2	189.14	1.76	Insignificant
Second Order Interaction					
AxBxC	11.14	2	5.57		Insignificant
Within	7718.57	72	107.20	0.05	
		83			

Table 4.61. Mean Values of Interest in Humanities

	A_1		A_2		
	B_1	B_2	B_1	B_2	
C_1	23.43	27.43	35.14	34.86	38.21
C_2	29.86	33.71	31.71	32.14	31.85
C_3	34.42	28.28	35.57	28.28	31.64
	29.23	29.81	34.14	31.76	

$A_1 = 29.52$ $B_1 = 31.68$

$A_2 = 32.95$ $B_2 = 30.76$

Table 4.62. Summary of 2×2×3 Factorial esign for Home Science Area of Educational Interest

Sources of Variation	*Sum of Squares*	*df*	*Mean Variance*	*F-ratio*	*Significance*
Main Effects					
A	6205.75	1	6205.76	62.09	Significant
B	138.86	1	138.86	1.38	Insignificant
C	1040.17	2	520.08	5.20	Significant
First order Interaction					
A×B	105.19	1	105.19	1.05	Insignificant
A× C	971.45	2	485.72	4.86	Significant
B × C	85.07	2	42.53	0.42	Insignificant
Second Order Interaction					
A×B×C	196.74	2	98.37	0.98	Insignificant
Within	7195.43	72	99.94		
		83			

Table 4.63. Mean Values of Interest in Home Science

	A_1		A_2		
	B_1	B_2	B_1	B_2	
C_1	11.28	19.28	40.14	37.14	27.02
C_2	18.28	26.43	41.86	43.86	32.61
C_3	32.43	30.71	38.28	40.28	35.42
	20.66	25.47	40.09	40.43	

$A_1 = 23.06$ $B_1 = 30.37$

$A_2 = 40.26$ $B_2 = 32.95$

Table 4.63(a). Testing Significance of the Levels of Factor C

Levels of Factor C	*N*	*Obtained 't' ratios*	*Required significant 't' ratio at 0.5 level*	*Significance*
C_1 vs. C_2	28	2.09	2.05	Significant
C_1 vs. C_3		3.15		Significant

The mean difference required for significance between any two parts of the levels of factor C should be 5.47 or more. 't' test was not applied on thepair C_2 vs. C_3 as the difference between the means of this pair was less than 5.47.

Table 4.63 (b). Testing Significance of the levels of A×C Interaction

Levels of A×C Interaction	*N*	*Obtained 't' ratios*	*Required significant 't' ratio at 0.5 level*	*Significance*
A_2C_2 vs. A_1C_1	14	5.16	2.45	Significant
A_2C_2 vs. A_1C_2		3.63		Significant
A_2C_3 vs. A_1C_1		4.49		Significant
A_2C_3 vs. A_1C_2		3.16		Significant
A_2C_1 vs. A_1C_1		4.37		Significant
A_2C_1 vs. A_1C_2		3.04		Significant
A_1C_3 vs. A_1C_1		3.05		Significant

The mean difference required for significance between any two pairs of the levels of A×C interaction should be 13.08 more, 't' values were not calculated for the remaining pairs as the mean differences between rest of the pairs were less than 13.08.

Table 4.64. Summary of 2x2x3 Factorial Design for Science Area of Educational Interest

Sources of Variation	*Sum of Squares*	*df*	*Mean Variance*	*F-ratio*	*Signific-ance*
Main Effects					
A	1.71	1	1.71	0.01	Insignificant
B	48.76	1	48.76	0.38	Insignificant
C	375.93	2	187.96	1.46	Insignifcant
First order Interaction					
A×B	100.76	1	100.76	0.78	Insignificant
A× C	410.64	2	205.32	1.59	Insignificant
B × C	167.31	2	83.65	0.65	Insignificant
Second Order Interaction					
A×B×C	120.88	2	60.44	0.47	Insignificant
Within	9250.29	72	128.48		
		83			

Table 4.65. Mean Values of Interest in Science

	A_1		A_2		
	B_1	B_2	B_1	B_2	
C_1	36.43	34.86	38.85	39.28	37.35
C_2	37.85	42	34	41.43	38.82
C_3	39.57	39	37.85	27.71	40.39
	37.95	38.62	36.9	36.14	

A_1= 38.28 B_1 = 37.42
A_2= 36.52 B_2 = 37.38

Table 4.66. Summary of 2x2x3 Factorial Design for Technology Area of Educational Interest

Sources of Variation	*Sum of Squares*	*df*	*Mean Variance*	*F-ratio*	*Significance*
Main Effects					
A	2870.01	1	2870.81	21.09	Significant
B	41.44	1	41.44	0.30	Insignificant
C	19.60	2	9.80	0.07	Insignifcant
First order Interaction					
A×B	364.58	1	364.58	2.67	Insignificant
A× C	30.45	2	15.22	0.22	Insignificant
B × C	141.45	2	70.72	0.52	Insignificant
Second Order Interaction					
A×B×C	24.60	2	12.30	0.09	Insignificant
Within	9798.57	72	136.09		
		83			

Table 4.67. Mean Values of Interest in Technology

	A_1		A_2		
	B_1	B_2	B_1	B_2	
C_1	29	31.57	24.43	17.57	25.64
C_2	30.57	35.14	21.22	20	26.68
C_3	32	31.71	23.57	14.71	25.75
	30.52	32.81	23	17.43	

A_1= 31.66 B_1 = 26.76

A_2 = 20.21 B_2 = 25.12

Significance of Means Difference in the Intellectual Commitment Scores in Relation to Sex and Zones

In this sub- section, the significance of means difference in the intellectual commitment scores in relation to sex and zones was studied. Two way analysis of variance technique was applied. 2 × 3 factorial design was prepared. All the sets were equated by randomly selecting ten cases from each set of the experimental design as given below:

Paradigm of Experiment

Sex	*Boys*		*Girls*
A	A_1		A_2
Zones	$Zone_1$	$Zone_2$	$Zone_3$
B	B_1	B_2	B_3

The outcomes of this hypothetical experiment have been presented in table 4.68 and 4.69.

Table 4.68. Summary of 2×3 Factorial Design for Intellectual Commitment

Sources of Variation	*Sum of Squares*	*df*	*Mean Variance*	*F-ratio*	*Significance*
Main Effects					
A	864.90	1	864.90	13.27	Significant
B	140.06	2	74.53	1.14	Insignificant
First order Interaction					
A×B	99.46	2	49.73	0.76	Insignificant
Within	5475.06	84	65.17		
		89			

Table 4.69. Mean Values of Intellectual Commitment Scores

	A_1	A_2	
B_1	70.93	74.33	72.63
B_2	68	74.73	71.36
B_3	70.27	78.73	74.5
	69.73		75.93

Significance of Means Difference in the Intellectual Commitment Scores is Relation to Types of School and Qualification of Father

In this sub-section, the investigator studied the significance of means difference in the intellectual commitment scores when type of school and qualification of father worked as independent at variables. As there were two independent variables to influence the criterion, two way analysis of variance technique was applied. 2×3 factorial design was prepared. All the sets were equated by randomly selecting fifteen subjects from each set of the experimental design given below;

Paradigm of Experiment

Types of School	*Govt. School*		*Private School*
A	A_1	Average	A_2
Qualification of father B	High Qualification B_1	Qualification B_2	Low Qualification B_3

The outcomes of this hypothetical experiment have been presented in tables 4.70 to 4.71

Table 4.70. Summary of 2×3 Factorial Design for Intellectual Commitment

Sources of Variation	*Sum of Squares*	*df*	*Mean Variance*	*F-ratio*	*Significance*
Main Effects					
A	15.21	1	15.21	0.23	Insignificant
B	144.20	2	72.10	1.10	Insignificant
First order Interaction					
A×B	28.29	2	14.14	0.21	Insignificant
Within	5508.80	84	65.50		
		89			

Table 4.71. Mean Values of Intellectual Commitment Scores

	A_1	A_2	
B_1	76.93	74.67	75.8
B_2	73.13	72.43	72.78
B_3	72.66	73.13	72.89
	74.24	73.42	

Significance of Means Difference in The Intellectual Commitment Scores in Relation to Intelligence and Socio-Economic Status

Another objective of the study was to study significance of means difference in the intellectual commitment scores of students in relation to intelligence and socio- economic status. To realise this objective, the investigator applied two way analysis of variance technique. 2×3 factorial design was prepared. All the sets were equated by randomly selecting seven subjects from each set of the experimental design given below:

Paradigm of Experiment

Types of School	*Govt. School*		*Private School*
A	A_1		A_2
Socio-Economics Status	High Socio-Economic Status	Middle Socio-Economic Status	Low Socio-Economic Status
B	B_1	B_2	B_3

The outcomes of this hypothetical experiment have been presented in tables 4.72 to 4.74.

Table 4.72: Summary of 2×3 Factorial design for Intellectual Commitment

Sources of Variation	*Sum of Squares*	*df*	*Mean Variance*	*F-ratio*	*Significance*
Main Effects					
A	632.59	1	632.59	12.86	Significant
B	1683.26	2	841.63	17.10	Significant
First order Interaction					
A×B	1136.27	2	568.1	11.54	Significant
Within	1770.86	36	49.19		
		41			

Table 4.73. Mean Values of Intellectual Commitment Scores

	A_1	A_2	
B_1	69.48	66.66	68.7
B_2	76.43	55.85	66.14
B_3	72.11	72.02	72.06
	72.67	64.84	

Table 4.73 (a). Testing Significance of the levels of Factor B

Levels of Factor B	*N*	*Obtained 't' ratios*	*Required significant 't' ratio at 0.5 level*	*Significance*
B_2 vs. B_3	14	2.23	2.16	Significant

The mean difference required for significance between any two pairs of the levels of factor B should be 5.72 or more. The 't' values were not calculated for rest of the pairs of the levels of factor B as the difference between the means of these pairs was less than the reported value of 5.72.

Table 4.74. Testing Significance of the levels of A×B Interaction

Levels of Factor A×B	*N*	*Obtained 't' ratios*	*Required significant 't' ratio at 0.5 level*	*Significance*
A_1B_2 vs. A_2B_2	7	5.50	2.45	Significant
A_1B_2 vs. A_2B_2		2.61		Significant
A_1B_3 vs. A_2B_2		4.35		Significant
A_2B_3 vs. A_2B_2		4.32		Significant
A_1B_1 vs. A_2B_2		3.64		Significant
A_2B_1 vs. A_2B_2		2.89		Significant

The mean difference required for significance between any two pairs of the levels of A×B interaction should be 9.16 or more. The 't' values were not calculated for rest of the pairs of the levels of A×B interaction as the difference between the means of these pairs was less than the stated value.

The Significance of Means Difference on Controlling Certain Variables

In this Section, the objective was to study the significance of means difference in the intellectual commitment scores of various groups of students after controlling the influence of other variables significantly related with them in the experimental design. Analysis of co-variance technique was used for the analysis of this section.

Significance of means Difference in the Intellectual Commitment Scores of High Achievers and Low Achievers on Controlling the Influence of Intelligence

In this section, the investigator studied the significance of means difference in the intellectual commitment scores of high achievers and low achievers after controlling the influence of intelligence. Fifty subjects were randomly selected from each set of the experimental design prepared as such:

Paradigm of Experiment

High Achievers		*Low Achievers*	
A		B	
Intelligence	Intellectual Commitment	Intelligence	Intellectual Commitment
X_1	Y_1	X_1	Y_1

The outcomes of this hypothetical experiment have been presented in the following tables:

Table 4.75. Summary of Analysis of Co-Variance

Sources of Variation	*Sum of Squares*	*df*	*Mean Variance*	*F-ratio*	*Significance*
Among Means	104.19	1	104.19	2.25	Insignificant
Within Groups	4482.65	97	46.21		

Tablé 4.76. Values of Adjusted Y means

Groups	*M*	M_X	M_Y	M_{YX} *(adjusted)*
A	50	49.34	72.52	72.16
B	50	28.58	70.4	72.58

GM_X 38.96 GM_Y 73.46

Significance of Means Difference in the Intellectual Commitment Scores of Boys and Girls after Controlling the Influence of Intelligence

In this sub-section, the investigator studied the significance of means difference in the intellectual commitment scores of boys and girls after controlling the influence of intelligence. Experimental design given below was set up for the treatment of dependent variable. One hundred subjects were randomly selected from each set of the experimental design.

Paradigm of Experiment

Boyx		*Girls*	
A		B	
Intelligence	Intellectual Commitment	Intelligence	Intellectual Commitment
X_1	Y_1	X_1	Y_1

The outcomes of this hypothetical experiment have been presented in the following tables:

Table 4.77. Summary of Analysis of Co-Variance

Sources of Variation	*Sum of Squares*	*df*	*Mean Variance*	*F-ratio*	*Significance*
Among Means	1720.24	1	1720.24	31.15	Significant
Within Groups	10878.84	197	55.22		

Table 4.78. Values of Adjusted Y Means

Groups	*M*	M_X	M_Y	M_{YX} *(adjusted)*
A	100	38.77	69.74	69.74
B	100	38.82	75.61	75.61

G_{MX} 38.79 G_{MY} 72.67

The Study of Relationships

In this section, the investigator estimated the strength of relationship of (i) each of the seven areas of educational interest, with the total and subject- wise academic achievement of high school students (ii) each of the seven areas of educational interest with the socio- economic status, intellectual commitment, and intelligence. The correlation co- efficient of predictors (introversion- extroversion, socio- economic status, intellectual commitment, intelligence and adjustment) with the criterion (academic achievement) as well as among the predictors were also calculated with a view to see which predictors were highly correlated with one another as well as with the criterion.

The coefficients of correlation were computed by Pearson's Product Moment method. The co-efficients of correlation were computed for boys and girls group separately. The obtained co- efficients of correlation are given in the following tables.

Table 4.79. Co-efficients of Correlation (Boys =250)

	English	*Math*	*Social Science*	*Hindi*	*Science*	*Total Acad*
Agriculture	–.41*	–.15	–.12	–.13	–.03	–.20*
Fine Arts	–.17*	–.13	–.08	–.12	–.10	.14
Commerce	.11	–.04	.04	.00	.00	–.02
Humanities	.12	–.04	.03	.06	.07	.25*
Home Science	–.17*	.20*	–.14	–.01	.07	.21*
Science	.05	.08	.00	–.03	. .04	.23*
Technology	.05	.07	.00	.06	..09	.22*

*Significant at .05 level.

Regression Analysis

Regression analysis is generally done to predict the most likely measurement in one variable from the known measurements in an

Table 4.80. Co-efficients of Correlation (Girls = 250)

	English	*Math*	*Social Science*	*Hindi*	*Science*	*Total Acad*
Fine Arts	.07	–.19*	.03	.07	.06	–.13
Commerce	.07	–.11	.09	.02	.03	–.08
Humanities	.20*	.04	.06	.10	.09	.29*
Home-Science	.27*	.20*	–.05	–.05	.05	.11
Science	.17*	.05	.06	.00	.14	.14
Technology	.01	.04	.04	–.01	.05	.13

* Significant at .05 level.

Table 4.81. Co-Efficients of Correlation (Boys = 250)

	Socio-Economic	*Intellectual*	*Intelligence Commitment*
Agriculture	–.15*	.03	–.12
Fine -Arts	.09	.09	.12
Commerce	.00	.05	.03
Humanities	.06	.07	.04
Home Science	–.27*	.05	–.20*
Science	–.06	.17*	.00
Technology	.07	.08	.04

* Significant at .05 level.

Table 4.82 Co-efficients of Correlation (Girls = 250)

	Socio-Economic	*Intellectual*	*Intelligence Commitment*
Agriculture	–.16*	–.01	–.10
Fine-Arts	.19*	.08	.07
Commerce	.05	.05	.03
Humanities	.04	.15*	.08
Home-Science	–.27*	.04	.25*
Science	.00	.04	–.01
Technology	.17*	.12	.11

* Significant at .05 level

other. The ability to predict from several variables considered simutaneously is studied in the theory of multiple regression analysis. In multifactor experiments, where each experimental factor is quantitative, it may be desirable to investigate the extent to which all the factor is quantitative, it may be desirable to investigate the extent to which all the factors considered simultaneously account for variance in Y. Furthermore, it may be important to be able to predict the value of Y, given the combinations of quantitative factors and levels of expereimental treatments administred to a subject.

One of the objectives of the study was to derive regression for X_7 (Academic Achievement) from the known measurements of X_1 to X_6 (introversion, extroversion, socio-economic status, intellectual commitment, intelligence and adjustment). The objective was to see the extent to which all predictors taken together would account for variance in the cirterion.

Table 4.83. Inter Correlations Between Predictors and Criterion (Boys = 250)

Variables	*Academic achievement*	*Introversion*	*Extraversion*	*Socio economic Status*	*Intellectual commitment*	*Intelligence*	*Adjustment*
	$X_7(C)$	X_1	X_2	X_3	X_4	X_5	X_6
X_7		.12	–.00	.26	.22	.51	.22
X_1	.12		–.04	.07	–.04	.03	.11
X_2	–.00	–.04		.02	.08	–.03	.25
X_3	.26*	.07	.02		.09	.45*	.32
X_4	.22*	–.04	.08	.08		.27*	.28
X_5	.51*	.03	–.03	.45*	.27*		.41*
X_6	.22*	.11	.25*	.32*	.28*	.41*	

* Significant at .05 level

The regression equation was derived by the Doolittle method of multiple regression equation. When there are more than three predictors for the criterion the Doolittle method is alwasy preferred. The Correlation matrix given in table 4.83 and 4.84 was utilized for the calculation of beta-coefficients. The regression weights were calculated from the beta co-efficients. The obtained regression weight have been shown in table 4.85 and 4.86.

Table 4.84. Inter Correlations Between Predictors and Criterion (Girls = 250)

Variables	*Academic achievement*	*Introversion*	*Extraversion*	*Socio Economic Status*	*Intellectual commitment*	*Intelligence*	*Adjustment*
	$X_7(C)$	X_1	X_2	X_3	X_4	X_5	X_6
A_7		.04	.01	.41	.29	.58	.33
X_1	.04		–.00	–.10	.09	–.06	.09
X_2	.01	–.00		.08	.16	.03	.33
X_3	.41*	–.11	.08		.28	.41	.30
X_4	.29*	.09	.16*	.28*		.20	.26
X_5	.58*	–.06	.03	.41*	.20*		.32
X_6	.33*	.09	.33*	.30*	.26*	.32*	

*Significant at .05 level

Table 4.85. Regression Co-efficients for Boys (N = 250)

Tests	*1*	*2*	*3*	*4*	*5*	*6*
Regression co-efficients	.290	.045	.036	.078	.392	.47

Table 4.86. Regression Co-efficients for Girls (N=250)

Tests	*1*	*2*	*3*	*4*	*5*	*6*
Regression co-efficients	.157	–.184	.158	.270	.412	.125

Regression equations for boys and girls

The following regression equations were derived for the boys and girls.

For Boys

$$X_7 = 5.145+.290x_1 \quad +.36x_3 \quad +.178x_4$$
$$+.392x_5 \quad + -.047\ x_6$$

For Girls

$$X_7 = -\ 7.874 + .157x_1 + -.184\ x_2 +.158\ x_3$$
$$+\ .270x_4 \quad +\ .412\ x_5 +.\ 125\ x_5$$

Whereas

X_7 = Academic Achievement to be predicted

X_1 to x_6 = scores in the predictors

Using this equation and information from sources in the six tests, the researcher could compute a predicted average acore (x_7) for every student in sample.

5

Discussion of Results

Introduction

Once the data have been collected and analysed, the researcher can then proceed with the stage of discussion of the results. The process of discussion is essentially one of stating what the results show? What are their meanings and significance? What is the answer to the original problem? Discussion of results is not a routine or a mechanical process. It calls for a careful, logical and critical examination of results obtained after analysis, keeping in view the limitations of the sample chosen, the tools selected and used in the study.

As discussed in the first chapter, the objectives of present investigation were to study the nature of distribution of educational interest and intellectual commitment scores, to determine the educational interest patterns of different categories of students, to study the significance of means difference in the educational interest and intellectual commitment scores of students of different categories, to study the strength of relationships between different variables and to set up regression equation for academic achievement. The results obtained on each objective are discussed in the following pages :

Distribution of Scores

The calculated D values enlisted in tables 4.1 and 4.2 reveal that the results were not significantly different from normal distribution at .05 level. The calculated D values of .02, .03, .01, .04, .02, .05, .05 and .02 are far less than the significant table value of .0608 at .05 level. Hence, the hypothesis of normal distribution was accepted. The educational interest and intellectual commitment scores were normally distributed among the population sample.

The Educational Interest Patterns

The educational interest patterns of different groups of students were determined on the basis of mean values obtained by groups of students on seven interest areas. The discussion is based on the analysis done in chapter IV.

Sex wise. The table 4.3 reveals that boys showed their liking for science, humanities, technology, agriculture, commerce, fine arts and home science in order of preference. They were more interested in science, humanities and technology and least interested in home science.

The girls showed their interest in home science, science, humanities, fine arts, agriculture, technology and commerce in order of preference. They were more interested in home science, science and humanities and least interested in commerce and technology.

The boys and girls differed for their interest in home science and technology. Whereas girls gave first preference to home science, it received seventh preference from the boys. Similarly girls were least interested in technology whereas boys gave second choice to technology. The results obtained were in agreement with the earlier findings of Sahoo (1981), Jersild and Tasch (1949), Carter and Strong (1933), Yum (1942), Strong (1945), Kuder (1939) and Traxler and Mecall (1951). Girls by nature are more fit for household jobs. No doubt, with the change in values girls have become vocational minded and are taking interest in scientific and commercial subjects as well, yet home management is primary responsibility of girls. The Indian society demands the girls to look after all household affairs whether they are working or non - working. Hence their interest in home science is natural. Moreover home science is becoming very popular subject of study. Most of the universities are offering it as a undergraduate and post-graduate programme. It is also an established fact that boys have more mechanical ability as compared to girls. The graphical representation of the interest patterns of boys and girls through bar graph is presented in figure-1

Zone-wise. It is evident from the table 4.4 that the students of Jammu division were more interested in science, humanities and technology and less interested in agriculture and home science. They were equally interested in commerce and fine arts.

The subjects of Udhampur- Kathua and Poonch- Rajouri gave their first preference to science. Both gave second, fifth, sixth and seventh preference respectively to home science, technology, commerce and fine arts. Agriculture received third preference from the subjects of Udhampur and Kathua and fourth preference from the subjects of Poonch and Rajouri. The students of Poonch and Rajouri gave third preference to humanities whereas it received fourth preference from the students of Udhampur and Kathua.

The subjects of three zones showed their more interest in science. It is due to the genuine reasons. With the rapid advancements in the field of science and technology, everyone is realising the need of science education and is interested to go in for science stream.

The major differences were among the subjects of three zones for their interest in agriculture and home science. Whereas agriculture received third and fourth preference from the subjects of Udhampur-Kathua and Poonch-Rajouri, it received last preference from the subjects of Jammu. In semi urban areas of Poonch Rajouri, Udhampur and Kathua, people may be having some cultivating land which is not possible in urban places like Jammu. The subjects of zone second and third were less interested in technology and more interested in home science as compared to zone one. The results were in agreement with the earlier findings of Rangaswamy (1958) . The graphical representation of the interest patterns of students of three zones through bar- graph is presented in figure 2.

Schoolwise. The Table 4.5 reveals that subjects of government schools liked science, homescience, humanities, fine arts, agriculture,

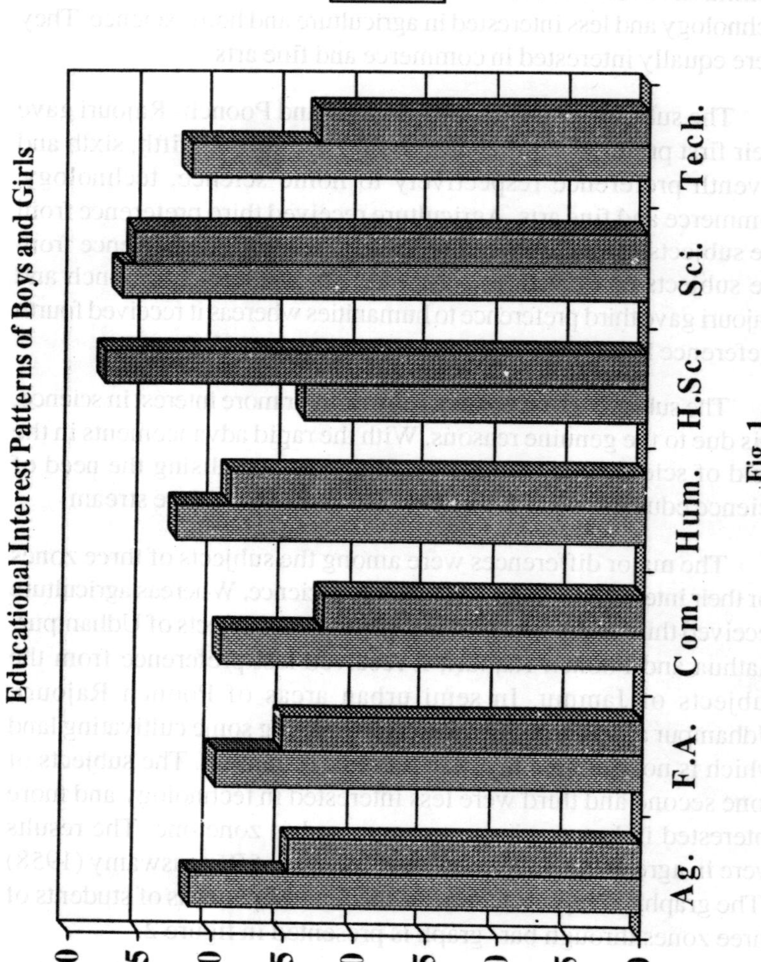
Educational Interest Patterns of Boys and Girls
Boys
Girls
40
35
30
25
20
15
10
5
0
Ag.
F.A.
Com.
Hum.
H.Sc.
Sci.
Tech.

Fig.1.

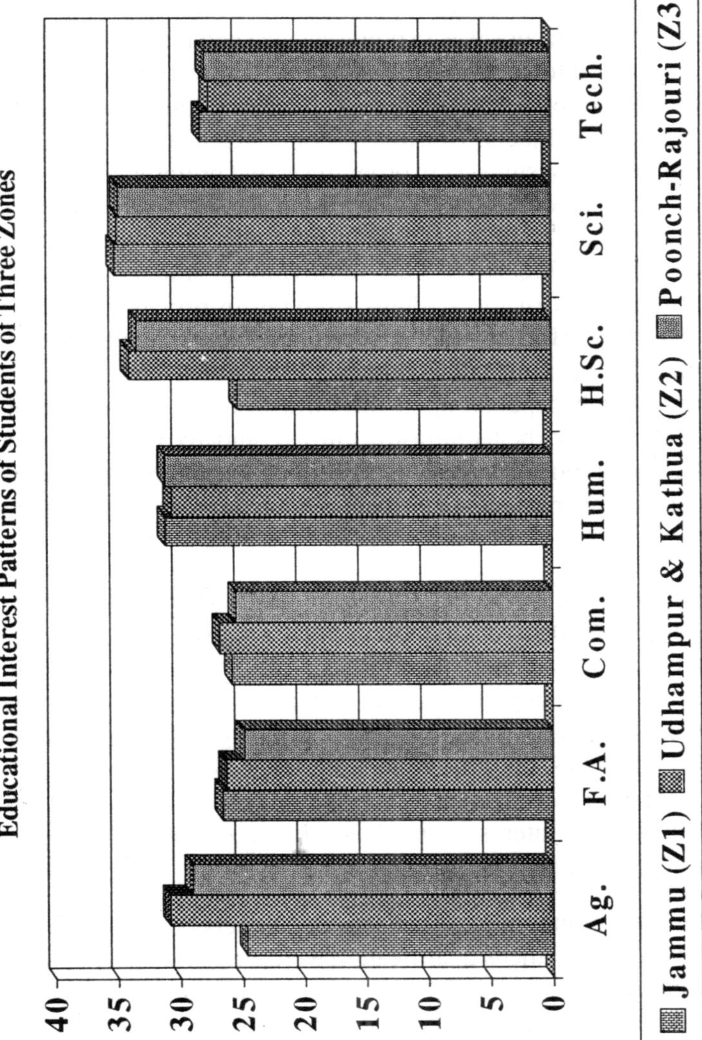
Educational Interest Patterns of Students of Three Zones
40
35
30
25
20
15
10
5
0
Ag.
F.A.
Com.
Hum.
H.Sc.
Sci.
Tech.
Jammu (Z1)
Udhampur & Kathua (Z2)
Poonch-Rajouri (Z3)

Fig. 2.

commerce and technology in order of preference whereas subjects of private schools liked science, humanities, technology, commerce, fine arts, home science and agriculture in order of preference. Both the groups showed first preference for science. The major difference between the two groups was in home science and technology areas of educational interest. Whereas subjects of government schools gave seventh preference to technology, it received third choice from private school subjects. Similiarly home science was liked by government school subjects in order of second preference whereas private school subjects were least interested in home science. Private schools especially train their students for competitive vocations of science and engineering. The achievement and intellectual commitment level of the students studying in private schools is generally high. Higher level of academic achievement is best guarantee for seeking admission to professional and technical institutes. Much depends upon the infrastructure of the school. Private schools have better infrastructure as compared to government schools. The graphical representation of interest pattern of students studying the government and private schools is presented in figure 3.

Qualification wise. From the table 4.6 it is evident that subjects belonging to high level of father's qualification liked science, humanities, homescience, technology, fine arts, commerce and agriculture in order of preference. The students belonging to average qualification level of father showed their liking for science, home science, humanities, fine arts, agriculture, technology and commerce in order of preference. The subjects belonging to low level of father's qualification were interested in science, home science, humanities, technology, commerce and agriculture.

The educational interest patterns of subjects belonging to the different levels of father's qualification were almost same with little deviations in agriculture and technology. The students belonging to high and poor qualification level of father were least interested in agriculture while it received fifth preference from the students belonging to average level of father's qualification. Likewise,

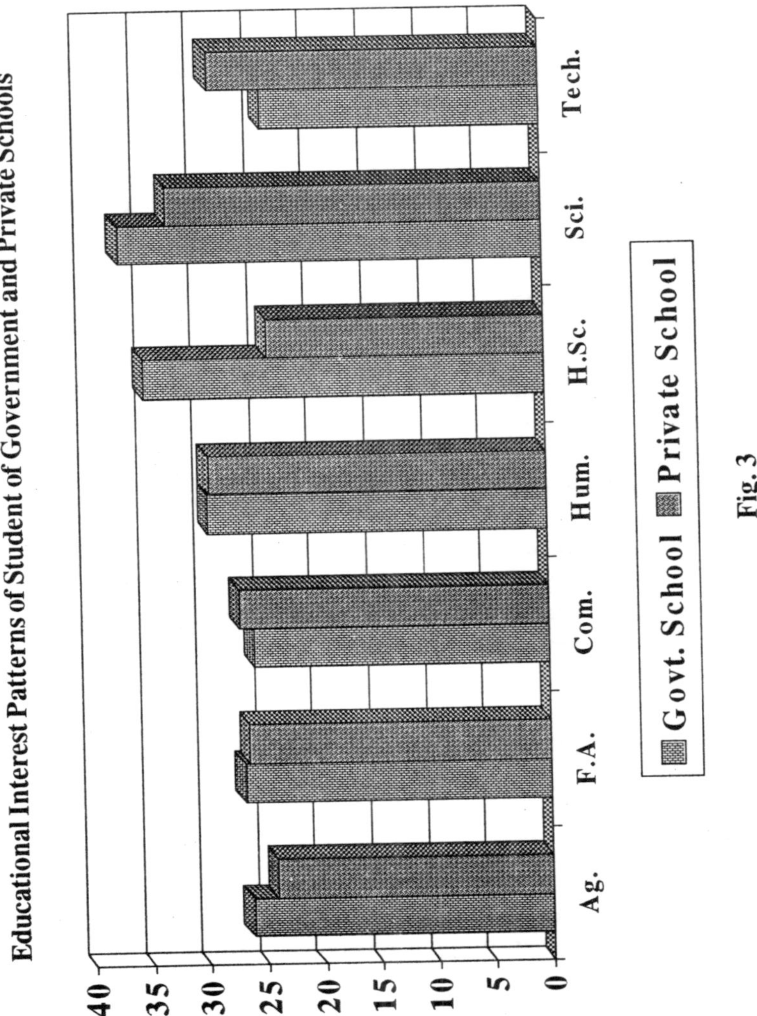
Educational Interest Patterns of Student of Government and Private Schools
40
35
30
25
20
15
10
5
0
Ag.
F.A.
Com.
Hum.
H.Sc.
Sci.
Tech.
Govt. School
Private School

Fig. 3

technology received fourth, fifth and sixth preference respectively from the students belonging to these three levels of father's qualification. The graphical representation of the interest patterns given in Figure 4.

Personality wise. Table 4.7 reveals that extroverted students showed their liking for science, humanities, home science, technology, commerce, fine arts and agriculture in order of preference whereas introverted students liked science, home science, humanities, commerce, technology, agriculture and fine arts in order of preference.

From the comparative judgement of the two groups, it was found that extroverted and introverted students were equally interested in science and they gave first preference to it. Subjects of both the groups were least interested in agriculture and fine arts. There was much commonness in both the groups for the rest of the interest patterns. The graphical representation of the interest patterns of extroverted and introverted students is given in figure 5.

Intellectual commitment wise. From the table 4.8 it clear that high intellectually committed students exhibited their preference for science, home science, humanities, technology, commerce, fine arts agriculture whereas low intellectually committed liked science, humanities, home science, technology, agriculture, commerce and fine arts in order of preference. Both the groups showed common liking for science and technology by giving first and fourth preference respectively. High intellectually committed students were least interested in agriculture whereas the choice of low intellectually committed students was at number five in order of preference for agriculture. The graphical representation of the interest patterns of high intellectually committed and low intellectually committed students through bar- graph is presented in figure 6.

Achievement wise. Table 4.9 reveals that high achievers were interested in science, humanities, technology, home science, commerce, agriculture and fine arts in order of preference. Low achievers were interested in home science, science, humanities,

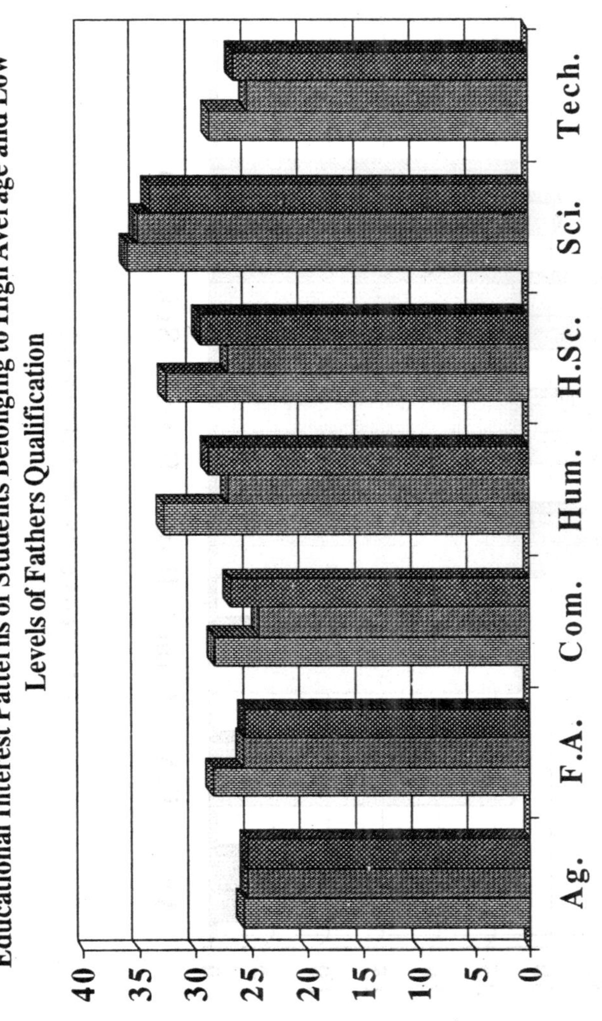
Educational Interest Patterns of Students Belonging to High Average and Low Levels of Fathers Qualification
40
35
30
25
20
15
10
5
0
Ag.
F.A.
Com.
Hum.
H.Sc.
Sci.
Tech.
High Qualification
Average Qualification
Poor Qualification

Fig. 4

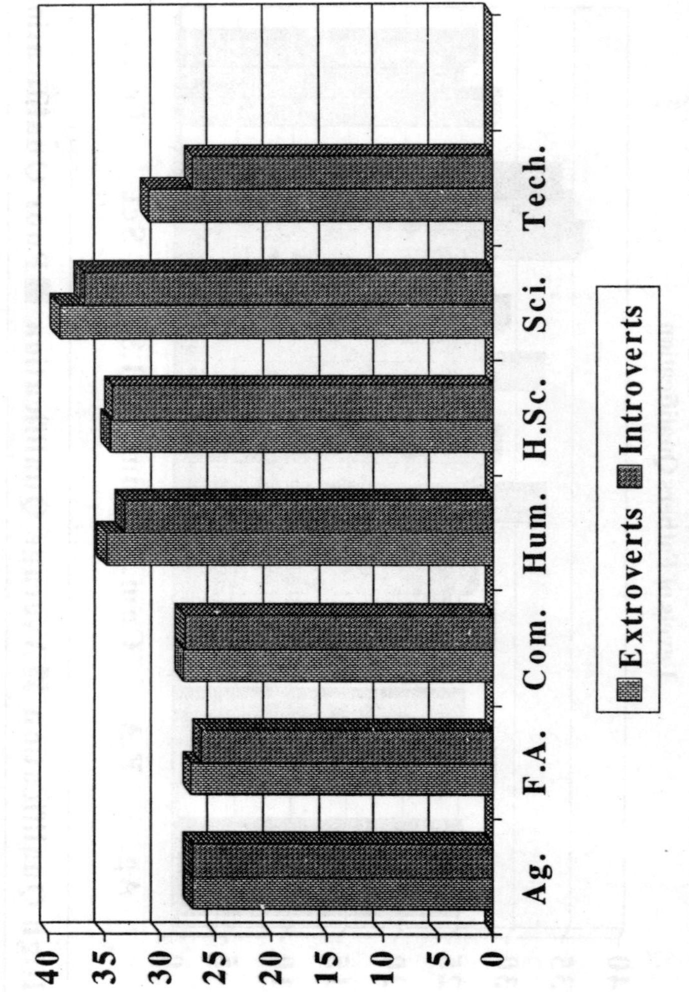
Educational Interest Patterns of Extrovert and Introvert Students
40
35
30
25
20
15
10
5
0
Ag.
F.A.
Com.
Hum.
H.Sc.
Sci.
Tech.
Extroverts
Introverts

Fig. 5

Educational Interest Patterns of High Intellectually Committed and Low Intellectually Committed Students

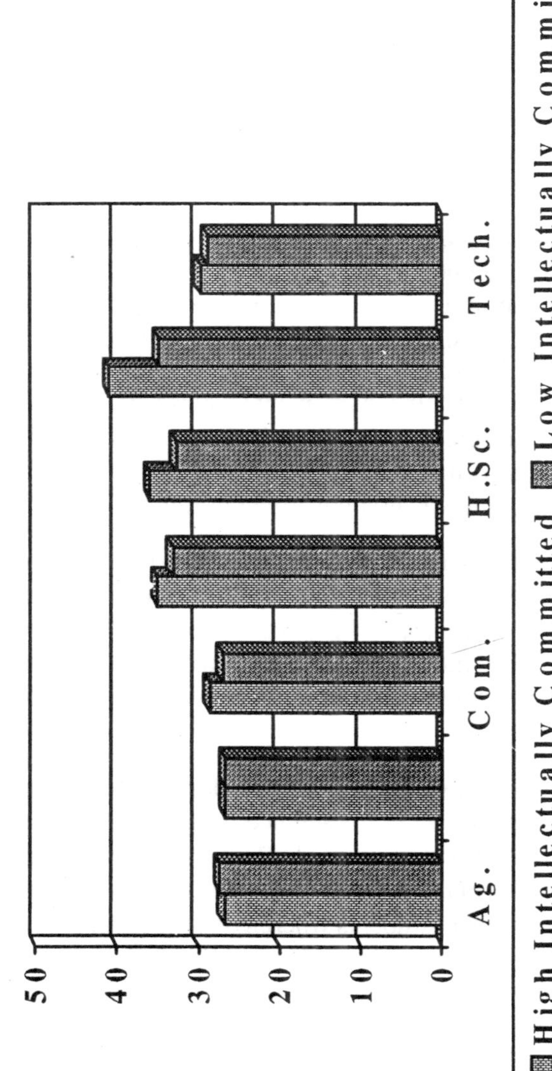

Fig. 6

commerce, fine arts, agriculture and technology.

Both the groups showed marked differences for some interest patterns. Whereas home science received fourth preference from the high achievers, it received first preference from the low achievers. Technology received third preference from the high achievers, whereas low achievers were least interested in technology. Both the groups were equally interested in agriculture. The results are not in line with the earlier findings of Vishnoi (1977).

The reasons of difference between the two groups for their liking of science and technology area are quite obvious. Higher percentage of marks is the first criteria of admission in medical colleges and technical institutes. University education in science subjects and mathematics also require higher merit. The low achievers cannot fulfil this criteria. Their achievement level is very low. Thus they do not aspire for science and technical education. The graphical representation of the interest patterns of high achievers and low achievers through bar- graph is given in figure 7.

Intelligence wise. From the table 4.10 it is evident that high intelligent students were more interested in science, humanities, home science, agriculture, technology commerce and fine arts in order of preference. Low intelligent students liked science, home science, humanities, agriculture, fine arts, commerce and technology in order of preference.

Both the groups showed common liking for some interest areas. Both showed first liking for science, fourth liking for agriculture and sixth liking for commerce. Differences between the two were found in the area of technology. Technology received fifth preference from high intelligent students whereas low intelligent students were least interested in technology. The graphical representation of the interest patterns of high intelligent and low intelligent is presented through bar- graph in figure 8.

Socio- economic status-wise. The table 4.11 reveals that the students of high socio- economic status group were interested in

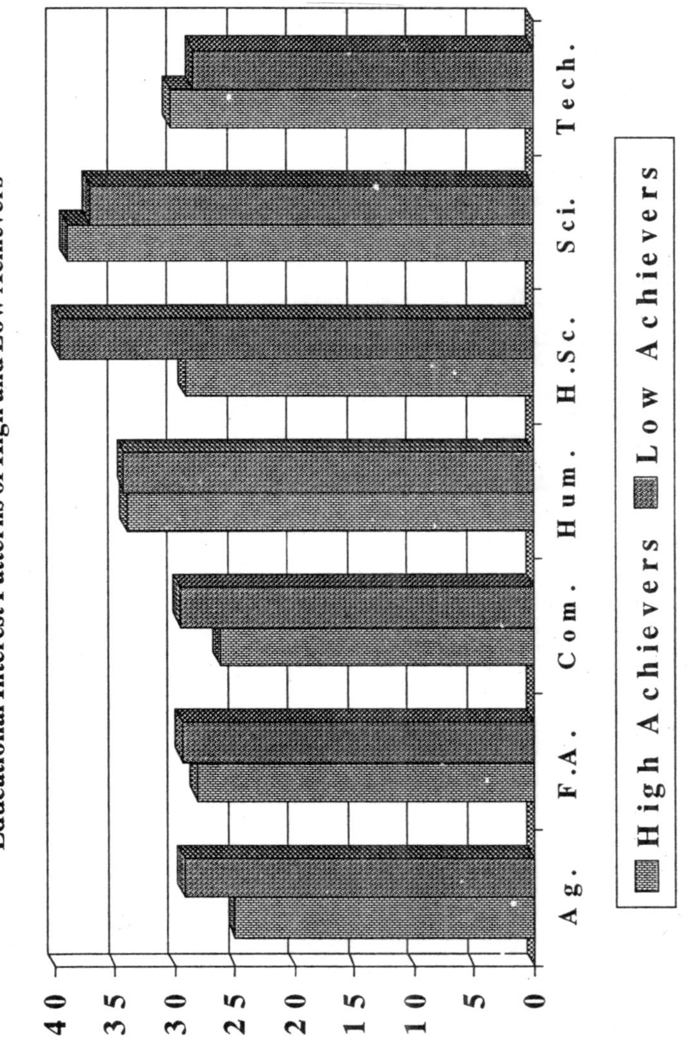
Educational Interest Patterns of High and Low Achievers
40
35
30
25
20
15
10
5
0
Ag.
F.A.
Com.
Hum.
H.Sc.
Sci.
Tech.
High Achievers
Low Achievers

Fig. 7

Educational Interest Patterns of High and Low Intelligent

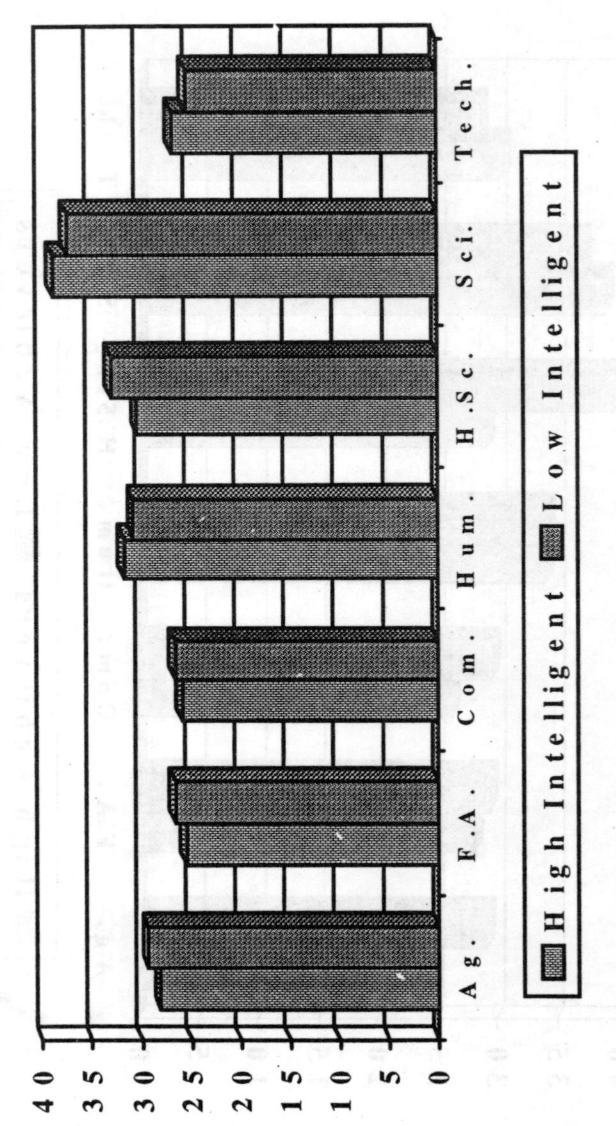

Fig. 8

science, humanities, homescience, technology, commerce, fine arts and agriculture in order of preference. They were more interested in science, humanities, home science and technology and least interested in fine arts and agriculture. The students of middle and low socio-economic status group liked science, home science, humanities and agriculture in order of preference. The subjects belonging to middle socio- economic status gave fifth preference to commerce whereas it received seventh preference from the low socio- economic status group. Both the groups gave sixth preference to technology.

Marked differences were found among the three groups for their interest pattern in agriculture area. Whereas students belonging to high socio- economic status were least interested in agriculture, middle and low socio- economic status group gave fourth choice for it. Similiarly middle and low socio- economic status groups were less interested in technology as compared to high socio- economic status group.

The concept of higher socio- economic status involves sound economic status, higher level of the education and occupation. Well off persons can never be supposed to work in fields and till land. In case they have farms, they can employ men and machines for cultivating land. Similiarly, the families whose members are highly educated and are placed in the higher occupational ladder generally prefer white collared jobs for their children. Thus, family background has definite influence on children's liking for various streams of education. Admission in professional colleges involves lot of expenditure. It requires intensive coaching. For seeking admission in professional colleges a huge amount is to be paid in the form of donations which the low socio- economic status groups can not afford. The graphical representation of the interest patterns of the students of high, middle and low socio- economic status group is given through bar graph in figure 9.

From the discussion made so far, it is evident that there was common liking of all the groups for Science. Modern age is the age of science. Scientific advancements are taking place very rapidly. No nation can think of progress without science education. Science

Educational Interest Pattern of Student Belonging to High, Middle and Low Level of Socio-Economic Status

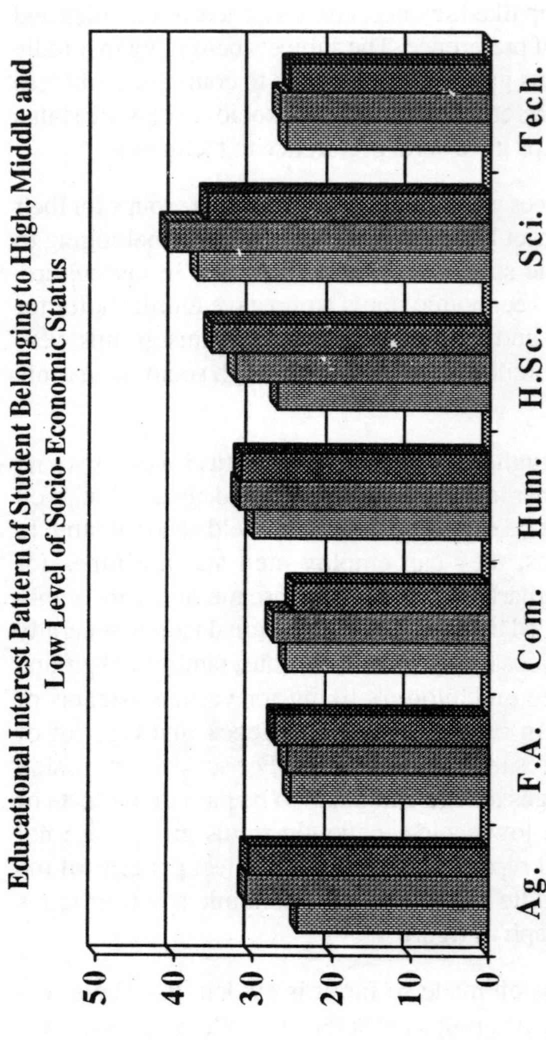

Fig. 9

education is necessary for changing the values and outlook of life. Realising the importance of science education, it has been made compulsory for all the students upto class x. New areas are explored in the field of science and it has greater scope as well. Therefore, every one is interested in science education irrespective of his abilities and limitations. The results obtained were in agreement with the earlier findings of Rangaswamy (1958), Arora (1955) and Pandey (1960).

Second liking of the students was for humanities. By virtue of natural endowments, some persons like such subjects which may have appeal to their emotions and represent the advancement of human civilization. They have more liking for theoretical subjects. Some students might have shown interest in humanities as secondary liking, i,e. they might be prepared to go for humanities stream in case their choice for science and engineering is not accepted, Moreover, our system of education lacks diversification of courses. All the persons cannot be accommodated by science stream with the result students develop liking for humanities. Again there is very high competition in science stream. Those students who lack ability of competition generally like arts subjects.

Significance of Means Difference

The analysis of variance was applied to study the significance of means difference in the educational interest and intellectual commitment scores of students in relation to different independent variables. The results obtained in chapter IV on various hypothetical experiments of means difference are discussed in the following sub-sections.

Significance of F - ratios in seven areas of educational interest in relation to sex and zones

The significance of obtained F - ratios in seven areas of educational interest in relation to sex and zones is discussed in this sub- section. The F- ratios against these two treatments and mean values of each area of educational interest are given in tables 4.12 to 4.25.

Main Effects A (Sex). The F - ratios given on tables 4.12, 4.16, 4.20, 4.24 were found to be significant for the main effect of factor A (sex) for agriculture, commerce, home science and technology areas of educational interest. The required significant value against df 1/84 is 3.95 at .05 level. The calculated value for agriculture was found to be 18.36, for commerce 13.19, for home science 51.93 and for technology 19.66. These values were greater than the required table value and hence were statistically significant. It could be interpretted that mean interest scores of boys and girls (A_1 and A_2), averaged over the levels of zone (B_1, B_2 and B_3) differed significantly in agriculture, commerce, home science and technology areas of educational interest. The hypotheses of no difference between boys and girls for their mean interest scores in these stated areas were rejected. There were 95% chances of obtaining the same results if the same experiment is repeated with the similar set of population.

On comparing the mean values of boys and girls given in tables 4.13, 4.17, 4.21, and 4.25 respectively, it could be interpreted that boys were more interested in agriculture, commerce and technology than girls as the mean value of boys in agriculture was 31.55, in commerce 29.53 and in technology 32.49 and those of the girls in agriculture was 24.68, in commerce 22.46 and in technology 23.22. The girls were more interested in home science than boys as their mean value in home science was 37.82 and those of boys was 23.95.

The calculated F- ratios given in tables 4.14, 4.18 and 4.22 for the main effect of factor A (sex) were found to be 0.18 for fine arts, 3.51 for humanities and 0.17 for science area of educational interest. These obtained F- ratios were not statistically significant. It could be interprested that the means of boys and girls, averaged over levels of B (zone) did not differ significantly in fine arts, humanities and science areas cf educational interest. The differences observed were due to mere chance. The hypotheses of no- difference between mean scores of boys and girls for these areas of educational interest were accepted. The findings of no difference between boys and girls for their mean scores in science area of educational interest were in agreement with the earlier findings of Pandey (1960) and Rothney (1937).

Main Effects B (Zone). The F- ratios for the main effect of factor B (Zone) were also found to be significant at .05 level for agriculture and home science areas of educational interest. The required significant value against df 2/ 84 is 3.11 at .05 level. The obtained F value for agriculture was 5.06 and for home science 4.48. These values exceeded the required table value. It could be inferred that there were significant differences in the agriculture and home science interest scores of students belonging to zone first, second and third averaged over the two levels of factor A (sex). The hypotheses of no significant difference between mean interest scores of students of three zones in agriculture and home-science areas were rejected. There were 95% chances of obtaining the same results in the replication of same experiment with the similar set of population.

Further on applying the 't' test on levels of factor B (Zone) in agriculture area of interest, it was found that the students of zone first and second differed significantly from each other for their mean interest scores as the 't' value given an table 4.13 (a) was found to be 3.11. The mean differences between zone first and third group and between zone second and third group did not reach the level of significance. These results showed that the significance of over all F for zones was due to significant mean difference only between zone first and second. It was interpreted that students of Udampur and Kathua having mean value of 30.73 as given in table 4.13 were are more interest in agriculture than the students of Jammu whose mean value is 24.7.

Application of 't' test on different levels of factor B in home science area of interest revealed that the students of zone first differed significantly from the students of zone second and third for their mean interest scores as the 't' values of these two pairs as given in table 4.21 (a) were found to be 3.69 and 3.57 respectively. The mean difference between zone second and third did not reach the level of significance. The results showed that the significance of overall F was due to significant mean difference between students of zone first and second and zone first and third. The second and third group did not differ significantly from each other. It could be interpreted that students of Udampur- Kathua and Poonch Rajouri having mean values of 34 and 33.37 respectively as given in table 4.29 were interested in home science than students of Jammu region whose mean value in home science was 25.3.

The tables 4.14, 4.15, 4.18, 4.22 and 4.24 revealed that the F-ratios for the main effect of factor B for fine arts area of interest were found to 0.35, for commerce 0.13, for humanities 0.02, for science 2.54 and for technology 0.04. These calculated F- ratios were not statistically significant. It could interpreted that the students of three zones averaged over the two levels of factor A (sex) did not differ significantly for their mean interest scores in fine arts, commerce, humanities, science and technology areas of educational interest. The hypothesis of no significant means difference in the interest scores of students of three zones in these areas of interest was accepted.

Interaction (A×B). From the table 4.12 it is evident that the F-ratio for the interaction effects of factor A and B for agriculture area of interest was found to be 4.83 which is significant at .05 level. It means sex effect (A) was not independent of zones (B) factor. In other words, the magnitude of the difference between A_1 and A_2 was not the same, within limits of random sampling for B_1, B_2 and B_3. The significance in the interaction was caused due to different levels of A and B. On comparison with permutation combination among different levels of A and B, the following combinations of levels were found to be contributing more towards the significance viz. $A_1 B_3$ vs. $A_2 B_3$, $A_1 B_3$ vs. $A_2 B_1$, $A_1 B_3$ vs $A_1 B_1$, vs. $A_2 B_2$, $A_1 B_2$ vs. $A_2 B_3$, $A_1 B_2$ vs $A_2 B_1$, $A_1 B_2$ vs $A_1 B_1$, $A_2 B_2$ vs $A_2 B_3$. The hypothesis of no significant interaction was rejected.

From the tables 4.14, 4.16, 4.18, 4.20, 4.22, 4.24 it is evident that the F-ratios for the interaction effects of factor A and B for fine arts area of educational interest were found to be 0.32, for commerce 0.93, for humanities 2.49, for home science 2.59, for science 0.57 and for technology 2.11. These calculated F-ratios were not statistically significant. It could be concluded that sex effect (A) was independent of the zone (B) factor. In other words, the magnitude of the difference between A_1 and A_2 was the same, within limits of random sampling, for B_1, B_2 and B_3 in the stated six areas of educational interest. The hypothesis of no significant interaction was accepted.

Significance of F- Ratios in Educational interest Areas in Relation to Type of School and Qualification of Father

The significance of obtained F- ratios in seven areas of educational interest in relation to two independent variables (type of school and qualification of father) is discussed in this section. The F- ratios against these two treatments and mean values of each area of educational interest are given in tables 4.26 to 4.39.

Main Effects A (Types of School). The F-ratios given in tables 4.34,4.36 and 4.38 were found to significant for the main effect of factor A (types of school) for homescience, science and technology areas of educational interest. The required significant value against 1/144 df is 3.91 at .05 level. The calculated value for home science area of educational interest was found to be 31.60, for science 6.63 and for technology 8.42. These obtained F- ratios were greater than the required table value and hence statistically significant. The results revealed that students studying in government and private schools averaged over the levels of factor (B) zone differed significantly for their mean interest scores in home science, science and technology areas of educational interest. The hypothesis of no significant difference in the mean educational interest acores of students studying in government and private schools for these stated areas was rejected.

On comparing the mean values of students of government and private schools given in tables 4.35 and 4.37, it could be interpretted that students studying in government schools were more interested in home science and science areas than students studying in private schools as the mean value of former in home science and science areas was 35.16 and 37.12 respectively and those of later was 24.33

and 32.82 respectively. Table 4.39 revealed that private school students having mean value of 29.03 in technology area were more interested in it than government school students whose mean value in technology area of interest was 24.44.

The calculated F- ratios given in table 4.26, 4.28, 4.30, and 4.32 for the main effect of factor A (types of school) for agriculture area were found to be 0.62, for fine arts 0.16, for commerce 0.64, for humanities 0.05. The obtained F- ratios were statistically insignificant. It could be interpretted that the mean interest scores of students studying in government and private schools, (A_1 and A_2), averaged over the levels of qualification of father, (B_1, B_2 & B_3) did not differ significantly in agriculture, fine arts, commerce humanities areas of educational interest. The hypothesis of no significant mean difference in the interest scores of these two groups of students in these stated areas was accepted.

Main Effects B (Qualification of Father). The F-ratio given in table 4.32 for the main effect of factor B(qualification of father) was found to be significant at .05 level for humanities area of educational interest. The required significant F- ratio against df 2/ 144 is 3.06 at .05 level. The calculated F - ratio of 5.71 was greater than the required table value. It could be interpretted that the students belonging to three levels of father's qualification, averaged over the two levels of factor A (types of school), differed significantly for their mean interest scores in humanities area of educational interest. The hypothesis of no- significant means difference was rejected.

Further on applying 't' test on different levels of factor B in humanities area of interest, it was found that students belonging to high level of father's qualification differed significantly from the students belonging to average and low level of father's qualification for their mean scores as the 't' values of these two groups given on table 4.33 (a) were found to 3.30 and 2.24 respectively. The mean difference between average and low qualification level did not reach the level of significance. The results showed that the significance of overall F was due to significant difference between high and average level of father's qualification group and between high and low level of father's qualification group. Group belonging to average and low level of father's qualification did not differ significantly from each other. It could be said that students belonging to higher level of father's qualification having mean value of 32.72 in humanities area were more interested in it than students belonging to average and middle level of father's qualification whose mean values in humanities area were 26.92 and 28.83 respectively as given in table 4.33. The students belonging to average and low level of father's qualification were equally interested in humanities.

The tables 4.26, 4.28, 4.30, 4.34, 4.36, and 4.38 revealed that the F- ratio for the main effect of factor B for agriculture area of interest was found to be 0.02, for fine arts 1.92, for commerce 2.51, for home science 2.75, for science 0.19 and for technology 1.47. These calculated F-ratios are statistically insignificant. It could interpretted that there were no significant means difference in the interest scores of students in agriculture, fine arts, commerce, home-science, science and technology areas so far as these levels of father's qualification are concerned. In other words, students belonging to three levels of father's qualification averaged over the two levels of factor A (types of school) were equally interested in agriculture, fine arts, commerce, home science, science and technology areas. The hypothesis of no significant means difference in these areas of educational interest in relation to independent variable (qualification of father) was accepted.

Interaction (A×B). From the table 4.28 (a) and 4.32 (a) it is evident that the calculated F- ratio for the interaction effect of factor A and B was found to be 3.06 for fine arts area and 4.00 for humanities area of educational significant. The calculated values were statistically significant. It means nature of difference between different levels of factor A and B in fine arts and humanities areas was not the same. The different levels of A and B have caused significance in the interaction. On comparison through the permutation combinations among different levels of A and B in fine arts area it was found that the following combination of levels contributed more towards the significance viz. $A_1 B_1$ vs. $A_1 B_3$, $A_1 B_1$ vs $A_1 B_2$ and $A_1 B_1$ vs. $A_2 B_1$.

For significant interaction of A and B in humanities areas of educational interest, the combination of levels $A_1 B_1$ vs. $A_1 B_3$, $A_1 B_1$ vs $A_2 B_2$ and $A_1 B_1$ vs $A_1 B_2$ contributed towards significance.

From the tables 4.26, 4.30, 4.34, 4.36 and 4.38 it is evident that the F- ratio for the interaction effect of factor A and B for agriculture area of educational interest was found to be 2.59, for commerce 1.60, for home science 0.65, for science 2.04 and for technology 1.50. These calculated F- ratios were statistically insignificant. It could be concluded that type of school (effect A) is independent of qualification of father (B factor). In other words, the magnitude of difference between A_1 and A_2 was the same, within limits of random sampling for B_1, B_2 and B_3 in agriculture, commerce, home science, science and technology areas of educational interest.

Significance of F- ratios in educational interest areas in relation to introversion- extraversion, intellectual commitment and academic achievement

The significance of obtained F- ratios in seven areas of educational interest in relation to three independent variables (introversion- extroversion, intellectual commitment and academic achievement) is discussed in this section. The F- ratios for each area of educational interest against these three treatments along with mean values are given in table 4.40 to 4.53 in chapter IV.

Main Effect A(Introversion/Extraversion). The tables 4.40, 4.42, 4.44, 4.46, 4.48, 4.50 and 4.52 revealed that the calculated F- ratios for the main effect of factor A (introversion- extroversion) for agriculture area were found to 0.00, for fine arts 0.14, for commerce 0.00, for humanities 0.26, for home-science 0.00, for science 0.56 and for technology 1.93. These obtained F- ratios were not statistically significant. It revealed that mean educational interest scores of extroverted and introverted (A_1 and A_2), averaged over the levels of intellectual commitment (B_1 and B_2) and academic achievement (C_1 and C_2) did not differ significantly in all the seven areas of educational interest. The hypothesis of no significant means difference in the educational interest scores of introverted and extroverted in seven areas of interest was accepted.

Main Effect B (Intellectual Comitment). The table 4.50 revealed that the F- ratios for the main effect of factor B (intellectual commitment) for science area of educational interest was found to be 4.20. The required significant F- ratio against df 1/47 is 4.04 at .05 level. The calculated F- ratio exceeded the required table value and hence was statistically significant. It could be interpretted that mean interest scores of high intellectually and low intellectually committed (B_1 and B_2), averaged over the levels of introversion-extroversion (A_1 and A_2) and academic achievement (C_1 and C_2), differed significantly in science areas of educational interest. There were 95% chances of obtaining the same results if this experiment was repeated with the similar set of population.

On comparing the mean values of high intellectually and low intellectually committed given in table 4.51, it could be said that high intellectually committed having mean value of 39 were more interested in science than the low intellectually committed who had value of 36.41 in science area.

The table 4.40, 4.42, 4.44, 4.46, 4,48 and 4.52 revealed that the F- ratio for the main effect of factor B for agriculture area were found to be 0.04, for fine arts 0.00, for commerce 0.33, for humanities 0.48, for home science 0.79 and for technology 0.08. These obtained F- ratios were not significant statistically. It could be stated that high intellectually committed and low intellectually committed scored equally in these areas of educational interest. The hypothesis of no significant means difference in the interest scores of high intellectually committed and low intellectually committed in the given areas of educational interest was accepted.

Main Effect C (Academic Achievement). From the tables 4.42 and 4.48 it is found that the F- ratios for the main effect of factor C (academic achievement) for fine arts area were found to be 4.60

and for homescience 8.54 against df 1/47. The obtained F- ratios were significant at .05 level. It could interpretted that there were significant means difference in the fine arts and home science interest scores of high achievers and low achievers, averaged over the two levels of factor A (extroversion-introversion) and two levels of factor B (Intellectual Commitment). The hypothesis of no significant mean difference was rejected.

On comparing the mean values of high and low achievers given in the tables 4.43 and 4.49, it can be said that low achievers were more interested in fine arts and home science than high achievers as the mean value of low achievers in fine arts and home science areas are 29.33 and 39.50 respectively and those of the high achievers in these areas are 24.16 and 29.04 respectively. This result showing the low achievers to be more interested in house hold activities were in agreement with the earlier findings of Vishnoi (1977). Similiarly, the results showing the low achievers to be móre interested in fine arts as compared to high achievers were not in agreement with the earlier findings of Vishnoi (1977).

The Tables 4.40, 4.44, 4.46, 4.50 and 4.52 revealed that the F-ratios for the main effect of C (academic achievement) for agriculture, commerce, humanities, science and technology areas of educational interest were found to be 2.09, 1.38, 0.00, 0.44 and 0.33 respectively. The obtained F- ratios were not significant. It could be interpretted that high and low achievers averaged over the two levels of factor A (Introversion-Extraversion) and two levels of factor B(Intellectual Commitment), did not differ significantly for their mean interest scores in agriculture, commerce, humanities, science and technology areas of educational interest. The hypothesis of no significant means difference was accepted.

Interactions (A×B), (A×C), (B×C) and (A×B×C) From the tables 4.40, 4.42, 4.44, 4.46, 4.48, 4.50 and 4.52 it is evident that the first order interactions A×B, A×C and B×C and second order interactions A×B×C were not significant for all the seven areas of educational interest. It could be concluded that introversion-extroversion effect (A) was independent of the intellectual commitment (B) and academic achievement (c) factors. Similiarly, intellectual commitment effect (B) was independent of the academic achievement (C) factor. And A,B and C effects were independent of one another.

Significance of F- ratios in educational interest areas in relation to sex, intelligence and socio- economic status

The significance of obtained F- ratios in seven areas of educational interest in relation to these independent variables (sex, intelligence and socio- economic status) is discussed in this section. The F- ratios for each area of educational interest against these three treatments along with means values are given in tables 4.54 to 4.67 in chapter IV.

Main Effect A (Sex). Table 4.58, 4.62 and 4.66 reveal that the F- ratios for the main effect of factor A (sex) for commerce, home science and technology areas of interest were found to be 5.90, 62.09 and 21.09 respectively. The required significant value against df 1/ 72 is 3.98 at .05 level. The obtained F- ratios were greater than the table value and hence significant. It could be interpretted that means of boys and girls (A_1 and A_2) averaged over the levels of intelligence (B) and socio economic status (C) differed significantly in commerce, homescience and technology areas of educational interest. The hypothesis of no- significant means difference was rejected.

On comparing the mean values of boys and girls given in tables 4.59, 4.63 and 4.67 respectively, it could be interpretted that boys were more interested in commerce and technology than girls as the mean values of boys in commerce and technology were 28.66 and 31.65 respectively and those of the girls were 23.67 and 20.21 respectively.

The girls were found to be more interested in home science than boys as the mean value of girls in home science was 40.26 and those of the boys was 23.06. The results showing the boys to be more interested in commerce as compared to girls were in agreement with the earlier findings of Rothney (1937).

The F- ratios for the main effect of factor A for agriculture, fine arts, humanities and science areas of educational interest were found to be 0.11, 1.63, 2.17 and 0.01 respectively. The F- ratios were not statistically significant. The non- significance of these F-ratios made the investigator to infer that the means of boys and girls, averaged over the levels of intelligence and socio- economic status, did not differ significantly in agriculture, fine arts, humanities and science areas of interest. The hypothesis of no- significant means difference was accepted.

Main Effect B (Intelligence). The table 4.54, 4.56, 4.58, 4.60, 4.62, 4.64 and 4.66 reveal that the F- ratios for the main effect of factor B (intelligence) for agriculture fine arts, commerce, humanities, home science, science and technology areas of educational interest were found to be 0.34, 0.25, 0.10, 0.19, 1.38, 0.38, and 0.30 respectively. These calculated F-ratios were not statistically significant, It lead the investigator to interpret that the means of high intelligent and low intelligent, averaged over the levels of sex and socio- economic status, did not differ significantly in all the seven areas of educational interest. The hypothesis of no significant means difference in these areas of educational interest was accepted. The results obtained were not in agreement with the earlier findings of Devi and Basavana (1985).

Main Effect C (socio-economic status). The table 4.54 and 4.62 reveal that the F- ratios for the main effect of factor C (socio-economic status) for agriculture and home science areas of interest were found to be 4.84 and 5.20 respectively. The required significant value against df 2/72 is 3.13 at .05 level. The calculated F- ratios were greater than table value and hence significant. It could be interpretted that means of students belonging to three levels of socio-economic status, averaged over the levels of intelligence and sex differed significantly in agriculture and home science areas of interest. The hypothesis of no significant means difference was rejected. There were 95% chances of obtaining the same results if the experiment was repeated with the similar set of population.

Further on applying 't' test on different levels of factor C in agriculture area of interest, it was found that high socio- economic status group differed significantly from middle and low socio-economic group for mean interest score in agriculture as the 't' values for each pair of combination were found to be 2.68 as given in table 4.55 (a). The means difference between middle and low levels of socio- economic status did not reach the level of significance. The results showed that the significance of overall F for socio- economic status in agriculture interest area was due to significant means difference only between high and middle socio-economic status group and between high and low socio- economic status group. The means of middle and low socio- economic status group did not differ significantly from each other. It could be interpretted that middle and low socio- economic status groups, each having mean value of 30.71 as given in table 4.63 were more interested in agriculture than high socio-economic status group whose mean value in agriculture was 24.31.

Application of 't' test on different levels of factor C in home-science area of interest, revealed that high socio-economic group differed significantly from middle and low socio- economic status group for mean interest scores in home science area as the 't' values of two groups given in table 4.63 (a) was found to be 2.09 and 3.15 respectively. The means difference between middle and low socio-economic status group did not reach the levels of significance. The results showed that the significance of overall F for socio- economic status in home science area was due to significant mean difference between high and middle socio-economic status group and between high and low socio-economic status group. The mean of middle and low socio- economic status group did not differ significantly from each other. It could inferred that high socio- economic status group having mean value of 27.02 as given in table 4.63 was less interested in home science than middle and low socio-economic status group whose mean values were 32.61 and 35.42 respectively.

The F- ratios for the main effects of factor C for fine arts, commerce, humanities, science and technology areas of educational interest were found to be 0.32, 0.52, 0.21, 1.46 and 0.07 respectively.

The obtained F- ratios were not significant. It made the investigator to infer that the means of high, middle and low socio- economic status group, averaged over the levels of sex and intelligence, did not differ significantly in these areas of educational interest. The hypothesis of no significant means difference was accepted.

Interaction (A×B). (B×C) and (A×B×C) : From the tables 4.54, 4.56, 4.58, 4.60, 4.62, 4.64 and 4.66 it is evident that the A × B, B × C first order interactions and second order interactions A × B × C were not significant for all the seven areas of educational interest. It could be interpretted that sex effect (A) was independent of the variable B (Intelligence). Intelligence effect (B) was independent of socio- economic status effect (C) . Further A,B and C effects were independent of one another.

Interaction (A×C). From the tables 4.64 and 4.62 it is evident that the F- ratios for the interaction effect of factor A and C in agriculture and home science areas of interest were found to be 9.69 and 4.86 respectively. These calculated values were statistically significant. It could be concluded that the sex effect (A) was not independent of socio- economic status (C). In other words, the magnitude of differences between A_1 and A_2 was not the same, withing limits of random sampling, for C_1 C_2 and C_3 in agriculture and home science areas of interest. The different levels of A and C factors caused significance in the interaction. On comparison through the permutation combinations among different levels of A and B in agriculture area, it was found that the following combination of levels contributed towards the significance viz. $A_1 C_3$ vs $A_1 C_1$ and $A_1 C_2$ vs $A_1 C_1$. For significant interaction of A and B in humanities area of interest, the combination of levels $A_2 C_2$ vs $A_1 C_1$, $A_2 C_2$ vs $A_1 C_2$, $A_2 C_2$ vs $A_1 C_1$, $A_2 C_2$ vs $A_1 C_2$, $A_2 C_1$ vs $A_1 C_1$, $A_2 C_1$ vs $A_1 C_2$ and $A_1 C_3$ vs $A_1 C_1$ were found to contribute towards the significance.

From the tables 4.66, 4.68, 4.60,4.64 and 4.66 it is evident that the F- ratios for the interaction effect of factor A and C in fine arts, commerce, humanities, science and technology areas of interest were found to be 1.73, 3.08, 1.91, 1.59, 0.11 respectively. The calculated

F- ratios were not statistically significant. It could be concluded that sex effect (A) was independent of socio- economic status (C) factor. In other words, the magnitude of difference between A_1 and A_2 is the same, with in the limits of random sampling, for C_1 and C_2 and C_3 in these five areas of educational interest.

Significance of F- ratios for intellectual commitment in relation to sex and zones

The significance of obtained F-ratios for intellectual commitment in relation to sex and zone is discussed in this section. The F- ratios against these two treatments along with mean values are given in table 4.68 and 4.69 in chapter IV.

Main Effects A (Sex). The table 4.68 reveals that the F- ratio for the main effect of A(sex) for intellectual commitment was found to be 13.27. The required significant value against df 1/84 is 3.95 at .05 level. The obtained F- ratios was greater than the table value and hence significant. It could be said that mean intellectual commitment scores of boys and girls (A_1 and A_2), averaged over the levels of zones (B_1,B_2 and B_3), differed significantly. The hypothesis of no significant means difference was rejected. The chances of not obtaining the same results in the replication of experiment. with similar set of population were only five in hundred.

On comparing the mean values of boys and girls given in table 4.69, it could be interpretted that girls were more intellectually committed than boys as the mean value of girl was 75.93 and those of boys was 69.73.

Main Effects B (Zone). From the same table it is evident that the F- ratio for the main effects of B (zone) was found to be 1.14. The required significant value against df 2/94 is 3.11 at .05 level. The obtained value was less than the table value and hence insignificant. It could be interpretted that mean intellectual commitment scores of students of zone first, second and third (B_1, B_2 and B_3), averaged over the two levels of sex (A_1 and A_2), did not differ significantly. The hypothesis of no significant means difference was accepted.

Interaction (A×B). From the same table, it is found that the F-ratio for the interaction effect of factor A and B was found to be 0.76 which was not significant. It could be concluded that sex effect (A) was independent of the zone (B) factor. In other words, the magnitude of differences between A_1 and A_2 was the same within the limits of random sampling for B_1,B_2 and B_3. The hypothesis of no significant interaction was accepted.

Significance of F- ratios for intellectual commitment in relation to types of school and qualification of father

The significance of obtained F-ratios for intellectual commitment in relation to type of school and qualification of father is discussed in this section. The F- ratios against these two treatments alongwith the mean values have been given in tables 4.70 and 4.71 in chapter IV.

Main Effect A (Types of School). The table 4.70 reveals that the F- ratio for the main effects of factor A (types of school) for intellectual commitment was found to be 0.23 which was insignificant against df 1/84 at .05 level. It could be interpretted that mean intellectual commitment scores of students studying in government and private schools (A_1 and A_2), averaged over the levels of qualification of father (B_1,B_2 and B_3), did not differ significantly.

Main Effect B (Qualification of Father). The same table reveals that the F- ratio for the main effects of factor B (qualification of father) was found to be 1.10 which was not significant against df 2/84 at .01 level. It could be interpretted that the mean intellectual commitment scores of students belonging to three levels of father's qualification (B_1 B_2 and B_3), averaged over the two levels of type of school (A_1 and A_2) did not differ significantly.

Interaction (A×B) From the same table, it is found that the F-ratio for the interaction effects of factor A and B was found to be 0.21 which was not significant against df 2/84. It could be concluded that type of school, effect (A) was independent of the qualification of father (B) factor.

The significance of F- Ratios for Intellectual Commitment in Relation to Intelligence and Socio- economic Status

The significance of obtained F- ratios for intellectual commitment in relation to intelligence and socio- economic status is discussed in this section. The F- ratios against these two treatments along with mean values have been given in table 4.72 to 4.74.

Main Effect A (Intelligence). The table 4.72 reveals that the F-ratio for the main effect A (intelligence) for intellectual commitment was found to be 12.86. The required significant value against df 1/36 was 4.12 at .05 level. The obtained F- ratio was greater than the table value and hence statistically significant. The significance of F- ratio made the investigator to infer that the mean intellectual commitment scores of high intelligent and low intelligent (A_1 and A_2), averaged over the levels of socio-economic status, (B_1, B_2 and B_3), differed significantly. The hypothesis of no significant means difference was rejected. There were 95% chances of obtaining the some results if the experiment was repeated with the similar set of population.

On comparing the means of high intelligent and low intelligent given in table 4.73, it could be inferred that high intelligent group was more intellectually committed than low intelligent as the mean value of high intelligent group was 72.67 and those of low intelligent group was 64.84.

Main Effect B (Socio-Economic Status). From the same table, it is evident that the F- ratio for the main effect of B (socio- economic status) for intellectual commitment was found to be 17.10. The required significant F- ratio against df 2/36 is 3.26 at .05 level. The obtained F- ratio was greater than the required value and hence statistically significant. It could be interpretted that mean intellectual commitment acores of high, middle and low socio- economic status group (B_1, B_2 and B_3), differed significantly. The hypothesis of no significant mean differences was rejected. The chance of not obtaining the same results were only five in hundred if the same experiment was repeated with the similar set of population.

Further on applying 't' test on different levels of factor B, it was found that low socio- economic status group differed significantly from middle socio- economic status group in mean intellectual commitment scores as the 't' value given in table 4.91 (a) was found to be 2.23. The mean differences between low and high socio- economic status group and between high and middle socio- economic status group did not reach the level of significance. The results showed that the significance of overall F for socio-economic status was due to significant mean difference only between middle and low socio- economic status group. The high socio-economic status group did not differ significantly from middle and low socio-economic status group. It could be interpretted that low socio-economic status group having a mean value of 72.06 as given in table 4.91 was more intellectually committed than middle socio-economic status group whose mean value is 66.14.

Interaction (A×B) From the table 4.72 it is evident that the F-ratio for the interaction effect of factors A and B was found to be 11.54 which was significant at .05 level against df 2/36. It means intelligence effect (A) was not independent of socio- economic status (B) factor. In other words, the magnitude of difference between A_1 and A_2 was not the same, within limits of random sampling for B_1, B_2 and B_3. On comparison with permutation combination among different levels of A and B, the following combination of levels contributed more towards the significance viz. $A_1 B_2$ vs $A_2 B_2$, $A_1 B_2$ vs. $A_2 B_1$, $A_1 B_3$ vs $A_2 B_2$, $A_2 B_3$ vs $A_2 B_2$, $A_1 B_1$ vs $A_2 B_2$ and $A_2 B_1$ vs $A_2 B_2$. The hypothesis of no-significant interaction was rejected.

The Significance of obtained F- Ratios on Controlling certain Variables

The analysis of co-variance technique was applied to study the significance of means difference in educational interest and intellectual commitment scores of different groups of students on controlling the influence of certain independent variables. The results obtained in chapter IV on various hypothetical experiments of means difference are discussed in the following sub- sections:

Significance of F- ratios for the intellectual commitment scores of high achievers and low achievers on controlling the influence of intelligence

The significance of obtained F- ratios for the intellectual commitment scores of high achievers and low achievers on controlling the influence of intelligence is discussed in this sub-section.

From table 4.75 it is evident that the adjusted F- ratio came out to be 2.25. The required significant value against df 1/97 is 3.94 at .05 level The obtained adjusted value was lesser than the table value and hence insignificant. It could be inferred that mean intellectual commitment scores of high achievers and low achievers did not differ significantly on controlling the influence of intelligence. The hypothesis of no significant difference in the mean intellectual commitment scores of high and low achievers on controlling the influence intelligence was accepted.

Significance of F- ratios of intellectual commitment scores of boys and girls on controlling the influence of intelligence

The significance of obtained F- ratio for the intellectual commitment scores of boys and girls on controlling the influence of intelligence is discussed in this sub- section.

From the table 4.77 it is evident that the adjusted F- ratio come out to be 31.15. The required significant value against df 1/197 is 3.89 at .05 level. The obtained F- ratio is greater than the required value and hence significant. Since the obtained F value exceeded the value of 3.89, it could be interpretted that the mean intellectual commitment score of the boys and girls differed significantly on partialling out the influence of intelligence.

Furthermore, it is evident from the table 4.78 that the adjusted mean of the intellectual commitment scores of boys and girls was 69.74 and 75.61 respectively. Since the mean of the girls was greater than that of the boys, it could be said that girls were more intellectually committed than boys even when the influence of intelligence was controlled.

Relationships

Pearson's Product Moment method was used to estimate the strength of relationship between some variables undertaken in the study. The results are discussed in the light of the analysis done in chapter IV. The discussion of the relationships is done in the following sub- sections.

Relationship of each of the seven areas of educational interest with the total and subject wise academic achievement

Correlation between seven areas of educational interest and each subject of study viz. english, math, social science, hindi, science and total academic achievement for the boys and girls, group has been discussed in this sub- section.

Boys Group. From the table 4.79 it is evident that there was a substantial negative correlation between interest in agriculture and achievement in english as the co-efficient of correlation came out to be -.41. It meant that high interest in agriculture was related to the low achievement in english or vice- versa. There were low negative correlation between some of the educational interests viz. fine arts and home science and achievement in english as the co- efficient of correlation came out to be -17, in each case. The obtained co-efficients of correlation though low were yet statistically significant. The hypothesis of zero population r was rejected. There were only five chances in hundred that a population r as large as -.41 and-.17 would arise from fluctuations of sampling. The co- efficients between some of the educational interest areas viz. commerce, humanities, science and technology and achievement in english were found to be .11, 12, .05 and .05 respectively. It meant there were negligible positive correlation between these stated educational interests areas and achievement in english.

From the same table it is evident that there was a low positive correlation between interest in home science and achievement in math as the coefficient of correlation was found to be .20. The obtained co-efficient was significant at .05 level. The hypothesis of zero population r was rejected. This meant that only five times in hundred trials a co-efficient as large as .20 would arise from accidents of sampling.

There was negligible positive correlation between some of the educational interest areas viz science and technology and achievement in math as the co- efficients of correlation given in table 4.79 were found to be .08 and .07 respectively.

From the same table it is evident that there was negligible negative correlation between some of the educational interest areas viz, agriculture, fine arts, commerce and humanities and achievement in math as the values given in table 4.79 were found to be -- .15, –.13, -.04 and -.04 respectively.

From the table 4.79 it is found that there was negligible negative correlation between some of the educational interest areas viz, agriculture, fine arts and home science and achievement in social science as the values were found to be –.12, -.08 and -.14 respectively. There was negligible positive correlation of the value of .03 and .04 between interest in commerce and humanities and achievement in social science. Moreover, there were no relationships between interest in science and technology and achievement in social science as the co-efficients were found to be .00 for each relationship. It meant distribution of the scores of two variables was independent of each other.

There was negligible negative correlation between some of the educational interests viz agriculture, fine arts, home science and science and achievement in hindi as the co- efficients given in table 4.79 was found to be -.13, -.12, -.01 and -.03 respectively. There was negligible positive correlation between interest in humanities and technology and achievement in hindi as the co- efficient of each relationship was found to be .06. Moreover, there was no relationship between interest in commerce and hindi as the co-efficient had come to be .00. It could be said that distribution of scores of two variables was independent of each other.

From the table 4.79 it was found that there was negligible positive correlation between some of the areas of educational interest viz. humanities, science and technology and achievement in science as the co- efficients of correlation were found to be .07, .04 and .09 respectively. Same table revealed that there was negligible negative correlation between interest in agriculture, fine arts and home science and achievement in science as the co- efficients were found to be -.03, -.10 and -.07 respectively. There was no relationship between humanities interest and achievement in science as the co- efficient of correlation was found to be .00. It could be concluded that dispersion of scores of interest in humanities and achievement in science was independent of each other.

From the table 4.79 it is evident that co- efficients of correlation between some of the educational interests viz, humanities, home science, science and technology and total academic achievement were found to be .25, .21, .23 and .22 respectively. It could be inferred that there were low positive correlation between these educational interests and academic achievement but the correlation coefficients were statistically significant at .05 level. On the formulated hypothesis of a population r of zero, therefore, only five times in hundred trials would positive rs of .25, .21, .23 and .22 arise through fluctuations of sampling.

The result showing low positive correlation of some of the interest areas with achievement was in agreement with the earlier findings of Gustad (1952), Melville and Frederiksen (1953), Darley and Hagenah (1955), Gowan (1957), Frankel (1960) and Geist (1961). The studies conducted by these persons reported that interests were related to academic achievement although obtained co- efficients of correlation were generally low.

The same table revealed that there was low negative correlation between agriculture interest and total academic achievement as the co- efficient was found to -.20, The obtained co- efficient was significant at .05 level. It meant that the distribution of scores was such that the high interest in agriculture was related to the low academic achievement or vice- versa. There was also negligible negative correlation of the value of -.02 between interest in commerce and total academic achievement.

Girls Group: From the table 4.80 it is evident that interest in agriculture and home science, each was having low negative correlation with achievement in english as the co-efficient of correlation in each case was found to be –.24 and –.27 respectively. It meant that distribution of scores was such as the high interest in agriculture and home science was related to the low academic achievement. The obtained co- efficients were also significant at .05 level. The hypothesis of zero population r in each case was rejected. There were only five chances in hundred that a population r as large as -.24 and -.27 would arise from fluctuations of sampling.

Again from the same table it is evident that interest in humanities and science, each was having low positive correlation with achievement in english as the co- efficient of correlation was found to be .20 and .17 respectively. The obtained co- efficients were significant at .05 level. Moreover, there was low positive correlation between some of the educational interest viz fine arts, commerce and technology and achievement in english as the co- efficients of correlation came out to be .07, .07 and .01 respectively.

The table 4.80 revealed that the interest in agriculture, fine arts and home science, each was having low negative correlation with achievement in math as the co- efficients of correlation came out to be -.23, -.19 and -.20 respectively. It could be interpretted that interest in agriculture, fine arts and home science was related to the low achievement in math. The obtained co- efficients were also significant at .05 level. The hypothesis of zero population r was rejected. There were only five chances in one hundred that a population r as large as -.23, -.19 and -.20 would arise from fluctuations of sampling. There was also negligible inverse relationship between interest in commerce and achievement in math as the co- efficient of correlation came out to be -.11. Moreover, there were negligible positive correlation between some of the educational interests viz. humanities, science and technology and achievement in math as the co-efficients of correlation came out to be .04, .05 and .04 respectively.

From the table 4.80, it was evident that the co-efficients of correlation between interest in agriculture and home science and achievement in social science came out to be -.10 and -.05 respectively. These co-efficients were too low to be statistically significant. This could be interpretted that there was negligible negative correlation between interest in agriculture and home science and achievement in social science. Again, from the same table it is revealed that there was negligible positive correlation between some of the educational interests viz fine arts, commerce, humanities, science and technology and achievement in social science as the co-efficients of correlation came out to be .03, .09, .06, .06 and .04 respectively.

From the table 4.80, it was evident that interest in agriculture and achievement in hindi were negatively correlated with each other. The co- efficient of correlation between the two variables come out to be -.20. The relationship though low, yet was significant at .05 level. The interest in agriculture was related with the low achievement in hindi or vice- versa. The hypothesis of zero population r was rejected and there were only five chances in hundred that population r as large as -.20 would arise from fluctuations of sampling. There was also inverse relationship between interest in science and achievement in hindi as the co- efficient of correlation came out to be -.05. But the correlation between the two variables was negligible.

From the same table, it was evident that there was negligible positive correlation of each educational interest area viz fine arts, commerce and humanities with achievement in hindi as the co-efficients in each case came out to be .07, .02, .10. Moreover there was no relationship between interest in science and technology and achievement in hindi as the co- efficients of correlation came out to be .00 and –.00 . It could be said that distribution of scores of two variables i.e. interest scores in science and achievement scores in hindi and interest scores in technology and achievement scores in hindi was independent of each other.

The table 4.80 revealed that the co-efficient of correlation between interest in agriculture and achievement in science came out to be -.18. It meant that there was a low inverse relationship between the two variables but the correlation was significant at .05. The interest in agriculture was related to low achievement in science or vice- versa. The hypothesis of zero population r was rejected. There were five chances in hundred that population r as large as -.18 or more would arise from fluctuations of sampling. Again there was negligible negative correlation of the value of -.06 between interest in fine arts and achievement in science.

The same table revealed that there were negligible positive correlation between some of the educational interest areas viz commerce, humanities, home science, science and technology and achievement in science as the co-efficients of correlation came out to be.03, .09, .05, .14 and .06 respectively. None of the obtained co-efficients was significant.

Table 4.80 revealed that there was low positive correlation between interest in humanities and total academic achievement and low negative relationship between interest in agriculture and total academic achievement as the co- efficients of correlation came out to be .29 and -.19 respectively. The obtained co-efficients were significant at .05 level. The hypothesis of zero population r was rejected. This meant that only five times in hundred trials would an r as large as .20 arise from accidents of sampling. The same table revealed that there was negligible positive correlation between some of the educational interests viz fine arts, home science, science and technology and total academic achievement as the co-efficients of correlation came out to be .13, .11, .14, and .13 respectively. There was negligible correlation between interest in commerce and total academic achievement as the co-efficient of correlation came out to be –.08.

Relationship of each of the seven areas of educational interest with socio-economic status, intellectual commitment and intelligence

Correlation between each of the seven areas of educational interest and socio- economic status, intellectual commitment and intelligence for the group of boys and girls have been discussed in this section.

Boys Group : From the table 4.81, it is evident that interest in agriculture and home science was having low negative correlation with socio-economic status as the co-efficients of correlation came out to be .-15 and .-27 respectively. The obtained co-efficients of correlation though low were yet statistically significant at .05 level. The hypothesis or zero population r was rejected. This meant that only five times in hundred trials would rs' as large as -.15 and .27 would arise from accidents of sampling. There was negligible negative correlation between interest in science and socio- economic status as the co-efficient of correlation came out to be -.06. The result showing negative correlation between interest in agriculture and socio- economic status was in agreement with the earlier findings of Samal (1977).

The same table revealed that co- efficients of correlation between interest in fine arts, commerce, humanities and technology and socio-economic status came out to be .09, .00, .06 and .07 respectively. It could be said that there were negligible positive correlation of the stated interest areas with socio-economic status. None of the correlations was statistically significant.

Table 4.81 revealed that there was low positive correlation between interest in science and intellectual commitment as the co-efficient of correlation was found to be .19. The obtained co-efficient was significant at .05 level. Interest in agriculture, fine arts, commerce, humanities, home science and technology, each was having negligible positive correlation with the intellectual commitment as the coefficients of correlation came out to be .03, .09, .05, .07, .05 and .08 respectively. None of the correlations was significant.

Table 4.81 again revealed that interest in home science was having low negative correlation with intelligence as the co- efficient of correlation came out to be -.20. It meant more interest in home science was related with the low intelligence or vice- versa. The obtained co- efficient was also significant at .05 level. It meant only five times in hundred trials an r as large as -.20 would arise from accidents of sampling. Moreover, there was negligible negative correlation between interest in agriculture and intelligence.

The same table revealed that there were negligible positive correlation between some of the educational interest areas viz. fine arts, commerce, humanities and technology and intelligence as the co- efficients of correlation came out to be .12, .03, .04 and .04 respectively. None of these stated interest areas were correlated significantly with the intelligence. Moreover, there was no relationship between interest in science and intelligence. The results of insignificant correlation of each of the interest areas with intelligence were in agreement with the earlier findings of Reed (1940), Samal (1970), Altender (1940) and Berdie (1945).

Girls Group : From the table 4.82, it is evident that there was low positive correlation between some of the educational interest areas viz fine arts and technology and socio- economic status as the co-efficients of correlation came out to be .19 and .17 respectively. There was low negative correlation between interest in agriculture and home science and socio- economic status as the co- efficients of correlation came out to be -.16 and -.27 respectively. All these obtained co- efficients though low were yet statistically significant at .05 level. The hypothesis of zero population r was rejected. It meant only five times in hundred trials would rs' as large as .19, .17, -.16 and -.27 would arise from fluctuations of sampling.

The same table revealed that interest in commerce and humanities was having low positive correlation with socio- economic status as the co- efficients of correlation came out to be .05 and .04 respectively. Moreover interest in science was not related with socio- economic status.

Again table 4.82 reveal that there was low positive correlation between interest in humanities and intellectual commitment as the co- efficient of correlation came out to be .15. The obtained co- efficient though low was yet significant at .05 level. The hypothesis of zero population r stood rejected and there were only five chances in hundred that the population r as large as .15 would arise from fluctuations of sampling. Again there was negligible negative correlation between interest in agriculture and intellectual commitment.

The same table revealed that there was negligible positive correlation between some of the educational interest areas viz. fine arts, commerce, home science, science and technology, and intellectual commitment as the co-efficients of correlation came out to be .08, .05, .04, .04 and .12 respectively.

It is evident again from the Table 4.82 that there was low negative correlation between interest in home science and intelligence as the co-efficient of correlation came out to be -.25. The obtained co-efficient was significant at .05 level. The hypothesis of zero population r was rejected. It meant that only five times in hundred trials an r as large as -.25 would arise from fluctuations of sampling. Moreover, there was negligible negative correlation between interest in agriculture and intelligence.

The same table revealed that some of the educational interest areas viz. fine arts, commerce, humanities science and technology, each had negligible positive correlation with intelligence. The co-efficients of correlation came out to be .07, .03, .08, .01 and.11 respectively which were not statistically significant.

Regression Analysis

The results obtained on regression analysis in chapter IV have been discussed in this section. The discussion is made in the following pages:

Regression weights of the predictors

Boys group. The calculated regression weights shown in table 4.85 in chapter IV indicated that intelligence and introversion were found to be the major contributors of academic achievement. The calculated value of regression weights for the intelligence and introversion came out to be .392 and .290 respectively. The regression weights for intellectual commitment, adjustment, extroversion and socio-economic status were found to be. 178, 047, .045 and .036 respectively.

Researches in the field of education have acknowledged the major contribution of intelligence in academic achievement. An intelligent person can understand and grasp the difficult concepts, has good memory, can solve problems more accurately and can reason well. All these mental abilities are prime movers of academic achievement.

Introverted persons generally remain busy with themselves. They stick to homes and spend no time in co- curricular activities with the result that they have ample time to pour over books. By nature they are studious. Thus introverted tendencies result in better academic achievement.

Intellectual commitment is another contributor in academic achievement though its contribution is low. Intellectual commitment is the tendency to be busy with academic activities. An intellectually committed spends much time in reading and studying and less in gossiping. By perseverance with the academic activities one is likely to achieve more even though one's intelligence is low. The hypothesis of no contribution of these predictors was rejected.

Academic achievement of the boys did not seem to be influenced by adjustment, extroversion and socio-economic status. The hypothesis of no contribution of these predictors to criterion was accepted.

Girls Group: The calculated regression weights for the girls group have been shown in table 4.86. In case of girls, regression weights against intelligence and intellectual commitment came out to be .412 and .270 respectively. The regression weights against extroversion, socio-economic status, introversion and adjustment were found to be -.184, -.158, .157 and .125 respectively.

In case of girls, intelligence and intellectual commitment were found to be the major contributors of academic achievement. The significance of intelligence, intellectual commitment and introversion has already been discussed. Five elements of adjustment were found to be contributing positively towards academic achievement. Better health, home, social, emotional and educational adjustment is congenial for good academic achievement. A mal-adjusted person is always frustrated and can not devote much to studies.

Better socio- economic conditions make positive contribution to academic achievement. These develop self- confidence in children. Children belonging to better socio- economic conditions are informed about the day-to-day happenings in the surroundings. They enjoy economic security which is a primary condition for good mental health. A mentally healthy person can devote himself more in studies than a mentally sick person.

The negative weight against the extroversion indicated that increase in extroverted tendencies affected academic achievement adversely. Extroverts are outgoing. They enjoy attending social functions and spend most of their time in co- curricular activities. They lack the temperament to pour over books for a good length of time. Thus they can not achieve high an academic achievement. The hypothesis of no contribution of predictors to academic achievement was rejected.

Multiple Regression Equation : The results of multiple regression equation made for the prediction of academic achievement are discussed as such :

Boys: From the regression equation for boys, it was found that a change of one unit raw score (+) in introversion, extraversion, socio- economic status, intellectual commitment, intelligence and adjustment brought a change of .290, .045, .036, .178, .392 and .047 units respectively on the raw scores of academic achievement of boys, i.e. as each introversion, extraversion, socio- economic status, intellectual commitment, intelligence and adjustment increases the academic achievement will also increase.

Girls: From the regression equation for girls, it was found that a change of one unit raw score (+) in intraversion, extraversion, socio-economic status, intellectual commitment, intelligence and adjustment brought a change of .157, -.184, .158, .207, .412 and .125 units on the raw score of academic achievement of the students, i.e. as each introversion, socio- economic status, intellectual commitment, intelligence and adjustment increases, academic achievement will also increase. The negative weight against the extraversion show that it acted as the suppressor variable for academic achievement. It means as extraversion increases, the academic achievement will decrease.

6

Findings, Educational Implications and Suggestions

Findings

In the light of the discussion of the results made in the previous chapter, the investigator derived the following findings:

Distribution of Scores

The scores of each of the seven areas of educational interest and intellectual commitment were normally distributed.

Interest Patterns

All the groups showed their common liking for science except girls and low achievers who gave second preference to it.

The students of Jammu region, boys group, private schools students and high achievers showed their interest in science, humanities and technology in order of preference.

The girls and low achievers showed their interest in home science, science and humanities in order of preference.

The students belonging to Poonch- Rajouri, government schools, average and poor level of father's qualification, introverts, high intellectually committed, low intelligent group and students from middle and low level of socio- economic status showed their liking for science, home science and humanities in order of preference.

The students belonging to high levelof father's qualification, extroverts, low intellectually committed, high intelligent group and students from high socio-economic status showed their interest in science, humanities and home science in order of preference.

The students of Udhampur and Kathua showed their liking for science, homescience and agriculture in order of preference.

Differences in Interest Patterns

Main effect A(sex) was found to be significant for agriculture, commerce, home science and technology areas of educational interest and insignificant for fine arts, humanities and science areas of educational interest. Boys were more interested in agriculture, commerce and technology and less interested in home science than girls.

Main effect B(zone) was found to be significant for agriculture and home science areas of educational interest and insignificant for fine arts, commerce, humanities, science and technology areas of educational interest. The students of zone first (Jammu) were less interested in agriculture than students of zone second (Kathua-Udhampur) and also less interested in home science than students of zone second (Kathua-Udhampur) and third (Poonch-Rajouri).

Interaction effect between A and B (sex and zone) was found to be insignificant for all the areas of educational interest except agriculture.

Main effect A (type of school) was found to be significant for agriculture, fine arts, commerce and humanities areas of educational interest and significant for home science, science and technology areas of educational interest. The students of government schools were more interested in home science and science and less interested in technology than students of private schools.

Main effect B (qualification of father) was found to be insignificant for all the areas of educational interest except humanities. Students belonging to high level of father's qualification were more interested in humanities than students belonging to average and poor level of father's qualification.

Interaction effect between A and B (type of school and qualification of father) was found to be significant for fine arts and humanities area of educational interest and insignificant for agriculture, commerce home science, science and technology areas of educational interest.

Main effect A (introversion- extraversion) was found to be insignificant for all the areas of educational interest.

Main effect B (intellectual commitment) was found to be insignificant for all the areas of educational interest except science area. High intellectually committed students were more interested in science than low intellectually committed students.

Main effect C (academic achievement) was found to be significant for fine arts and home science areas of educational interest and insignificant for agriculture, commerce, humanities, science and technology areas of educational interest. High achievers were less interested in fine arts and home science than low achievers.

Interaction effects between A and B, A and C, B and C and A, B and C were found to be insignificant for all the areas of educational interest.

Main effect A (sex) was found to be significant for commerce, homescience and technology areas of educational interest and insignificant for agriculture, fine arts, humanities and science areas of educational interest. Boys were more interested in commerce and technology and less interested in homescience than girls.

Main effect B intelligence was found to be insignificant for all the areas of educational interest.

Main effect C socio-economic status was found to be significant for agriculture and homescience areas of educational interest and insignificant for fine arts, commerce, humanities, science and technology areas of educational interest. Students belonging to high socio-economic status were less interested in agriculture and home science than students of middle and low socio- economic status.

Interactions between A and B, B and C and A, B and C were insignificant for all the areas of educational interest except A×C which was significant only for agriculture and home science areas of educational interest.

Differences in Intellectual Commitment

Main effect A (sex) was found to be significant for intellectual commitment. Girls were more intellectually committed than boys.

Main effect B (zone) and interaction effect between A and B was found to be insignificant for intellectual commitment.

Main effect A (type of school), B (qualification of father) and interaction effect between A and B (type of school and qualification of father) was found to be insignificant for intellectual commitment.

Main effect A (Intelligence) was found to be significant for intellectual commitment. High intelligent students were more intellectually committed than low intelligent students.

Main effect B (socio-economic status) was found to be significant for intellectual commitment. Students belonging to low socio-economic status were more intellectually committed than students belonging to average socio- economic status group.

Interaction effect between A and B was found to be significant for intellectual commitment.

Differences in Intellectual Commitment on Controlling.

There was no significant means difference in the intellectual commitment scores of high and low achievers on controlling the influence of intelligence.

Means difference in the intellectual commitment scores was not independent of sex when intelligence was controlled.

The means difference in the educational interest scores was independent of levels of academic achievement when intellectual commitment was controlled except in home science area. Low achievers were found to be more interested in home science than high achievers.

Relationships

Achievement in english was found to have significant negative relationship with agriculture, fine arts, home science interests in case of boys and with agriculture and home science interests in case of girls. Achievement in english was having significant positive correlation with interest in humanities and science in case of girls.

Achievement in math was found to have significant negative relationship with interest in home science in case of boys and with agriculture, fine arts and homescience interests in case of girls.

Achievement in hindi and science was found to have significant negative relationship with agriculture interest in case of girls.

Total academic achievement was found to have negative relationship with agriculture interest both in case of boys and girls and significant positive relationship with humanities, home science, science and technology interests in case of boys. In case of girls also total academic achievement was having significant positive relationship with humanities.

Socio- economic status was found to have significant negative relationship with agriculture, home science interests in case of boys and with agriculture, fine arts, home science and technology interests in case of girls.

Intellectual commitment was found to have significant positive relationship with science interest in case of boys and with humanities interest in case of girls.

Intelligence was found to have significant negative relationship with home science interest both in case of boys and girls.

Regression Analysis

Intelligence and introversion were found to be the major contributors towards academic achievement of boys. Intelligence and intellectual commitment were found to be the major contributors towards academic achievement of girls.

Educational Implications

The following implications were stated in reference to the above findings for the parents, teachers, curriculum planners, guidance workers and counsellors and state for education of the children.

The educational interests play very significant role in educational and vocational guidance. Educational guidance is the process of helping the students to develop and accept an integrated and adequate picture of himself and a clear understanding of his problems, and of his role in the world of education (school and college), with satisfaction to himself and benefit to the society. It usually happens in the schools where no guidance programmes exist, that pupils choose such subjects for the study which have no or little relationship with their vocational goals and ambitions, with the result they become misfit. This breeds educational failure, dropout and maladjustment which consequently promotes wastage and stagnation in high school. Whether the child is learning in school or is trying to carve out a career for himself, or is engaged in building up relationship of personal-social nature to live a happy corporate life, there is a need for educational, vocational, personal and social guidance. There must be provision for guidance programme in the school time table. In every school, there should be guidance programme under the charge of an expert psychologist so as to understand the students, i.e. their abilities, aptitudes, interest and personality patterns through intelligence tests, aptitude tests, personality tests, interest inventories and cumulative records and to provide educational, vocational and psychological guidance.

The doctrine of interest of education means that the learning can not take place without interest and, therefore, the interest of the learner should play an important part in deciding the content and method of instruction for different categories of students. But, even an adequate curriculum will not give desirable results unless the actual lessons are planned accordingly. The teachers while planning the lessons should keep the interests of different categories of students in view. This way students will find interest in their lessons and will derive pleasure in cooperating with the teachers.

Besides, certain personality characteristics, achievement level and mental abilities are necessary for achieving success in particular educational and vocational course. The teacher should have knowledge about the basic traits and abilities of the students and accordingly guide them to choose a course or career.

The study has implications for parents as well. The parents generally complain of the low achievement of their wards. They should understand the educational, vocational needs of their children in the light of their abilities and other required characteristics and help them to their adjustment and wholesome development.

Interests seem to develop out of satisfying activity and they tend to stimulate further activity. Learning is derived from the same experiences and is directly influenced by the enthusiasm a child has for the process. School curricula of today should be complete with material that furnish many possibilities for interest to develop. The curricula of high school and college should contain samples of many life situation so that the students may find several interesting elements in it. Moreover the teachers should adopt those methods of teaching which develop and maintain interest of the students in the subject.

Suggestions for Further Research

- The study can be conducted to study the interest patterns of college students.
- The interest patterns can be studied in relation to certain other non- cognitive variables like achievement motivation, locus of control and cognitive variable like creativity etc.
- The interest patterns of rural students can also be studied and rural-urban comparison can be made.

- Interest patterns of students of different castes can also be studied.
- Interest patterns of students belonging to different categories of father's occupation can be studied.
- The study can be conducted at the state level as well.

Bibliography

Allport, G.W. (1938). *Personality—A Psychological Interpretation.* New York : Halt, Rinehart and Winston Inc.

Altender, L.E. (1940). The Value of Intelligence, Personality and Vocational Interests Tests in a Guidance Programme. *Journal of Educational Psychology,* 31, 449-450.

Anastasi, A. (1967). *Psychological Testing.* New York: The MacMillan Company.

Arora, H.L. (1955). An Investigation into the Hobbies and Curricular Activities of Adolescent Students. *Educational and Psychological Studies.*

Blustein, D.L. and Flum, H. (1999). *A Self Determination Perspective of Interests and Exploration in Career Development.* Palo Alto, CA : Davies Black Publishing.

Berdie, R.F. (1945). Ranges of Interests. *Journal of Applied Psychology.* 39, 268-281.

Best, J.W. (1977). *Research in Education.* New Delhi: Prentice Hall of India Pvt. Ltd.

Biswas, A. and Aggarwal, J.C. (1971). *Encyclopaedic Dictionary and Directory of Education.* New Delhi: The Academic Publishers.

Box,G.E.P. (1953). Non-normality and Tests on Variance. *Biometrica,* 15, 318-335.

Brown, F.G. (1976). *Principles of Educational and Psychological Testing.* New York: Holt, Rinehart and Winston.

Burt, C. (1962). Relationship between Ability and Attainment. *British Journal of Educational Psychology,* 15, 28-29.

Carter, H.D. (1932). Twin Similarities in Occupational Interests. *Journal of Educational Psychology,* 38, 641-655.

Carter, H.D. and Strong, E.K. (1933). Sex Differences in the Occupational Interests of High school Adolescents. *Journal of Psychology,* 12, 166-173.

Chatterji, S. (1978). Chatterji's Non-language Preference Record Examiner's Manual Form 1962. Calcutta : *Indian Statistical Institute.*

Chauhan, S.S. (1978). *Advanced Educational Psychology.* New Delhi : Vikas Publishing House Pvt. Ltd.

Cronbach, Lee, J. (1984). *Essentials of Psychological Testing.* New York : Harper and Row.

Darley, J.G. and Hagenoh, T. (1955). *Vocational Interest Measurement.* Minneapolis : University of Minnesota Press.

Delano, Omobolade O. (1995). Factors that Influence Educational Aspirations of Yoruba Youth in Nigeria. *Dissertation Abstracts International,* 53(9), 239.

Devi, G. Nalni and Basavana, M. (1985). A Study of Interests in Relation to Intelligence and Socio-economic Factors among College Students. *Journal of Institute of Educational Research,* 9(3) 56-60.

Dubin, R. (1975). Central Life Interests and Organizational Commitment of Blue Collar and Clerical Workers. *Administrative Science Quarterly,* 20, 411-421.

Dutt, M. (1952). An Investigation into the Relationship Between Interest and Achievement. Unpublished M.Ed dissertation, C.I.E., Delhi.

Edwards,Allen L. (1971) *Experimental Design in Psychological Research.* New Delhi : Amerind Publishing Co. Pvt. Ltd.

English, H.B and English, A.C. (1958). *A Comprehensive Dictionary of Psychological and Psychoanalytical Terms.* Toronto : Longman's, Green and Company.

Faunce, W. (1959). *Occupational Involvement and Selective Testing of Self-esteem.* Paper presented at the Meeting of the American Sociological Association, Chiago.

Ferguson,G.A. (1985). *Statistical Analysis in Psychology and Education.* New York : McGraw Hill International Book Co.

Fisher, R.A. (1935). *The Design of Experiments.* London : Oliber and Boyd.

Garret, H.E. (1981). *Statistics in Psychology and Education.* Bombay : Vaklis Feffer and Simons Pvt. Ltd.

Geist, H. (1961) An Explanatory Study of the Relationship between Grades and a Pictorial Interest Test. *California Journal of Educational Research,* 12, 91-96.

Good, C.V. (1959). *Dictionary of Education.* New York. Columbia University Press.

Gowan, J.C. (1957). Intelligence, Interest and Reading Ability in Relation to Scholastic Achievement. *Psychological News Letter,* New York University, 85-87.

Guilford, J.P. (1965). *Fundamental Statistics in Psychology and Education.* New York : McGraw Hill Book Co.

Gustad, J.W. (1952). Academic Achivement and Strong Occupational Level Scores. *Journal of Applied Psychology,* 35, 75-78.

Gustad, J.W. (1954). Vocational Interests and Socio-economic Status. *Journal of Applied Psychology,* 38, 336-338.

Hawes, G.R. and Hawes, L.S. (1982). *The Concise Dictionary of Education.* New York : Van Nostrand Reinhoid Company.

Hmingthanzula (2002) : A Study of Vocational Interest and Occupational Aspirations of Class X Students of District Headquarters of Mizoram as Related to SES and Academic Achievement. *Indian DissertationAbstracts,* 95-96.

Jalota, S.S. (1976). *Group Test of General Mental Ability : Manual.* Delhi : Manasayan.

Jalota, S.S., et al., Comp. (1970). *Socio-economic Status Scale Questionnaire (Urban) : Manual.* New Delhi : The Psycho-Centre.

Jersild, A.T. and Tasch, R.J. Comp. (1949). *Children's Interests and What they Suggest for Education.* New York : Teachers' College.

Kundu, C.L. (1985). *Educational Psychology.* New Delhi : Sterling Publishers Pvt. Ltd.

Kuppuswami, B. (1974). *Manual of Socio-economic status Scale.* New Delhi : Mansayan.

Lodhal, T.M. and Kejner, M. (1965). The Definition and Measurement of Job-involvement. *Journal of Applied Psychology,* 49, 24-33.

Lawler, E.E. and Hall D.T. (1970). Relationship of Job Characteristics to Job Invlovement, Satisfaction and Intrinsic Motivation. *Journal of Applied Psychology,* 44, 305-312.

Mehren, W.A. and Lehman, I.J. Comp. (1973). *Measurement and Evaluation in Educational Psychology* : New York : Holt Rinehart and Winston.

Melville, S.B. and Frederiksen, N. (1952). Achievement of Freshmen Engineering Students and the Strong Vocational Interest Blank. *Journal of Applied Psychology,* 36, 160-173.

Misra, K.M., (1990) Vocational Interests of Secondary School Student. *Journal of Education and Psychology,* 48(1-2).

Mosier, C.I. (1941). A Short Cut in the Estimation of Split-halves Co-efficients. *Educational Psychological Measurement,* 1, 407-408.

Panda, B.N. (1994). A Study of Vocational Interests and Academic Performance of Tribal Adolescents. *Journal of Psychological Researches,* 38(3), 25-27.

Pandey, B.R. (1960). *Our Adolescents, their Interests and Education.* Unpublished Ph.D. Thesis, Lucknow : Department of Psychology, Lucknow University.

Patchen, M. (1970). *Participation Achievement and Involvement on Job.* Englewood Cliff, NJ : Prentice Hall.

Pathak, K.C. (1978). Effect of Family Background on the Development of Interests. *Psychological studies,* 23.

Rangaswamy, C.S. (1958). *An Investigation into the Interests of High School Pupils in Mysore State.* Research Section,Teachers' College, University of Mysore.

Rastogi, K.G. (1963). Interests, Intelligence and Achievement of High School Students. *Guidance Review,* 3(4).

Reed, H.B. (1940). The Relation of Bernseuter Personality and Thurstone Vocational Interest Scores to each other and to Scholastic and Mechanical Achievement. *Psychological Bulletin,* 37, 449-450.

Renee, P. (1994). African American Eighth Graders: Factors Affecting their Educational and Ocupational Aspirations. *Dissertation Abstracts International,* 42(11) 177.

Rossi, B. Hummel (1975). The Determinants of intellectual Commitment in University Students. *Character Potential,* 7(4).

Rotham Phillip (1954). Socio-economic Status and the Values of Junior High School Students. *The Journal of Educational Sociology,* special issue, 26.

Rothney, J.W.R. (1953). A Statistical Analysis of an Alumni Survey. *Journal of Genetic Psychology,* 52, 215-234.

Sahoo, P.K. (1980). Vocational Preferences of 10th Grade Boys and Girls. *Experiments in Education,* 13(2).

Saleh, S.D. and Hosek, J. (1976). Job involvement : Concept and Measurement. *Academy of Management Journal,* 19, 213-224.

Savickas, M.L. (1999). *The Psychology of Interests.* Palo Alto, CA : Davies Black Publishing.

Saxena, M.C. (1980). *Vayaktitva Parakh Parashnaveali : Manual.* Delhi : Central Bureau of Educational and Vocational Guidance, Department of Psychological Foundations.

Sharma K. and Verma, B.P. (1991). Educational and Vocational Interests. *Indian Journal of Psychometry and Education,* 22(2).

Sharma, S. (1956). An Investigation into the Interests of Adolescent Girls of Delhi. *Educational and Psychological Studies.*

Singh, L. (1959). An Investigation into the Vocational Interests of High School Boys of Churu Distt. *Journal of Educational Psychology.*

Singh, Y. and Singh, H.M. (1981). *Personality Inventory : Manual.* Agra : National Psychological Corporation.

Srinivas, Chitra (1979). *Faculty Leadership Styles and Intellectual Commitment among College Students.* Unpublished M. Phil Dissertation, New Delhi : Zakir Hussain Centre for Edcuational Studies, Jawahar Lal Nehru University.

Stoddard, G.D.(1943). *The Meaning of Intelligence.* New York : MacMillan and Co. Ltd.

Strong, E.K. (1943). *Vocational Interests of Men and Women.* Standford, Calif : Standford University Press.

Strong, E.K. (1938). *Strong Vocational Interest Blank for Men : Manual.* Palo Alto Calif : Consulting Psychologists Press.

Terman, L.N. and Miles, C.C. (1936). *Sex and Personality.* New York : The MacMillan and Co.

Thorndike, R.L. (1944). Interests and Abilities. *Journal of Applied Psychology,* 28, 43-53.

Thorndike,R.L. (1977). *Early interests, their Performance and relation to Abilities.* New York : The MacMillan Company.

Townsend, A. (1954). Achievement and Interest Ratings for High School Boys. *Educational Research Bulletin,* 49-54.

Traxler, A.E. and Macall, W.C. (1951). Some Data on the Kuder Preference Record. *Educational Psychological Measurement,* 3, 339-355.

Tyler, L.E. (1951). The Relationship of Interests to Abilities and Reputation among First Grade Children. *Educational Psychological Measurement,* 11, 215-264.

Tuckey, J.W. (1949). Comparing Individual Mean in the Analysis of Variance. *Biometrics,* 99-144.

Vishnoi, Kusum (1977). Interests Patterns of High and Low Achievers : A comparative study. *Indian Educational Review,* 12(1), 44-48.

Verma, R. (1965). *An Introduction to Edcuational and Psychological Research.* New Delhi : Asia Publishing House.

Vroom, V. (1962). Ego Involvement, Job Satisfaction and Job Performance. *Personal Psychology,* 15, 159-177.

Warner, Schaie, E.K. (1958). Occupational Level and the Primary Mental Abilities. *Journal of Educational Psychology,* 49, 292-303.

Wiseman, S. (1954). Raven Interest Test. *British Journal of Educational Psychology,* 24, 95-101.

Yadav, Raj Kumar (2000). A Study of Relationship between Socio-economic Status and Vocational Preferences of Adolescents in the Ahirwal Region of Haryana. *Journal of All India, Association for Educational Research,* 12(3&4), 41-46.

Yum, K.S. (1942). Students Preference in Divisional Studies and their Preferential Activities. *Journal of Psychology,* 13, 193-200.

Zargar, A.H. and Matoo, M.I. (1993). Creative Thinking Ability and Vocational Interests. *Journal of Psychological Researches,* 37(3), 47-50.

Index

❑❑❑